DREAM DEALER: STUART WALKER AND THE AMERICAN THEATER

DREAM DEALER: STUART WALKER AND THE AMERICAN THEATER

JoAnn Yeoman

Star Cloud Press
Scottsdale, Arizona
2007

Dream Dealer: Stuart Walker
and the American Theater

Copyright © 2007
by JoAnn Yeoman

Cover art by Alan Tongret

Cover Design by Trish Hadley

All rights reserved. No part of this book may be used
or reproduced in any manner whatsoever without written permission
from the publisher, except in the case of brief quotations
embodied in articles and reviews.

Published by

~ STAR CLOUD PRESS ~

6137 East Mescal Street
Scottsdale, Arizona 85254-5418

ISBN: 978-1-932842-22-7
Paperback $ 14.95

StarCloudPress.com

Library of Congress Control Number: 2006938333

Printed in the United States of America

To Alan

Table of Contents

Introduction	i
Chapter One — Getting Out	1
Chapter Two — The Theatre That Comes to You	15
Chapter Three — America's Best Plays, America's Best Actors	31
Chapter Four — The Stock Tradition	56
Chapter Five — Almost Home	62
Chapter Six — Hollywood Denouement	73
Epilogue — Memory	81
Chapter Notes	84 — 99
Appendix I — Indianapolis Stock Company	103 — 110
Appendix II — Cincinnati Stock Seasons	113 — 121
Bibliography	122 — 138
Acknowledgments	139
About the Author	141 — 142
Index	143 — 150

An unidentified sketch of Stuart Walker most probably rendered in the early 1930's. Billy Rose Theatre Division, The New York Public Library for the Performing Arts, Astor, Lenox, and Tildon Foundations.

INTRODUCTION

I love the introductions to books, especially biographies. I'm always interested in why writers choose to spend so much time with a person, often one who is, like Stuart Walker who died in 1941, no longer available for interviews.

I came to discover Stuart Walker while visiting a home in Augusta, Kentucky which was situated on the Ohio River only a block away from his birthplace. A local resident who knew of my work in the professional theater showed me a few old Portmanteau clippings and I recognized this man — not the man himself you understand, but in him the men and women I've known all my life. Gifted individuals who work hard every day, take nothing for granted, and risk all for a single passion.

What struck me immediately was that he was the definition of successful but not necessarily famous — and that is true of most of my friends and colleagues in the profession whom I admire and love. Success in this business means that you are able to make a living, feed your family, earn the respect of your peers, and continue to be employed in the theater throughout your life. And although Walker had his share of public attention during his lifetime I would hardly call him famous. Fame is a benchmark that means more to those outside the profession. Fame has more to do with luck, a carefully orchestrated image, a tragic death or, occasionally, even genuine talent. Fame is Marilyn Monroe, Michael Jackson and, thank heaven, Laurence Olivier.

I was also drawn to Walker because, in addition to sharing a Zodiac sign (Pisces), we also share a philosophy of theater that focuses on the essential qualities of a good script and a gifted cast rather than the aspects of spectacle that more often than not distract from good material, camouflage bad material or betray a lack of trust in the material on the part of the director. He also believed that the audience was an indispensable part of the performance. He believed both in trusting and obligating them. Me too.

Another of his goals and great enjoyments was the training of young actors and for the last ten years I too have had that pleasure while working with students at Arizona State University who are studying theater, dance and music.

I was intrigued as well by Walker's weaknesses, his vulnerabilities, his volatile nature, his mercurial outbursts. Walker's idiosyncrasies and unashamed passions were often endearing; his personality was full of dichotomies and he had a terrible habit of speaking (or rather writing) before he thought through the consequences of his statements. I'm afraid we share that too.

Most importantly I believe that his core qualities will speak to anyone who wants to succeed no matter the choice of profession. He was a mega-dreamer who was smart enough to know that only he could make those dreams come true and he was courageous enough to take the risks necessary in their pursuit. I wish you sweet dreams and I wish for you the courage to follow them.

> "It may be that we are all engaged in the profession of dreams, for it is always the hope of tomorrow, the vision, the dream, we are waiting for." Stuart Walker

Chapter One: Getting Out

STUART WALKER WAS A SMALL-TOWN BOY. He grew up in a rural area which in the late 19th Century was more active than it is today. But even a small town that provides a window to the outside world is still just that: a place to be from, a place to feel nostalgia for, a place to talk about in interviews once you're safely settled elsewhere.

The Ohio River Valley is without a doubt picturesque and evocative of more romantic and less complex times. Walker was born and lived the first ten years of his life in one of its loveliest spots, Augusta, Kentucky, 49 miles southeast of Cincinnati. His old home on Riverside Drive still stands facing the Ohio; its front door only a few steps from the river and, in landmark years, only a few hours from the legendary and catastrophic floods that seem to occur with regularity. Like most families that treasure the coming of the dogwood blossoms, the sight of the great blue heron, or the soundless wake of the ferry boat, the Walkers were steeped in the traditions of their home town.

Just across the river is Ripley, Ohio, which partnered with Augusta in providing an underground escape route for slaves. This song from the mid-19th Century resonates:

> Where the great big river
> Meets the little river
> Follow the Drinking Gourd.
> The old man is waiting for to carry you to freedom,
> If you follow the Drinking Gourd. (Anonymous)

Freedom within plain sight. Stories of heroism, selflessness, narrow escapes and tragic failures were part of Augusta's mid-19th century river history. The first Methodist college in the country was founded in Augusta and, like many other buildings preserved by a community restoration project, is still on the top ten sights of the tourist beat. Stephen Foster's sister, Henrietta, and his uncles, Joseph and John Tomlinson, all lived in Augusta and tradition holds that Foster wrote *My Old Kentucky Home* while visiting them. Music consistently played an important part in all incarnations of Stuart Walker's companies and it's likely that as a child he took pride as well as inspiration knowing that such an international talent as Foster had created one of his songs just a few doors away from the Walker's.

Gospel music was also an accessible form to him. Although there is no record of the Walker family's registration at any local church, it's not much of a stretch to imagine young Stuart becoming interested in the music-filled, energy-propelled services of the local black Methodist Church that had its own congregation. The vigor of the music, the theatricality of the ceremony, the collaboration of the whole congregation and the charismatic preaching styles would have made an impression on him. He could certainly hear the songs coming from the small building on Bracken Street and when the congregation spilled out onto the lawn he was literally in heaven. After all, the rituals of early religion and the elements of the theater are historically closely related.

Much of Augusta's architecture and layout remain the same as they were during Walker's boyhood. What has altered, of course, is the role Augusta played as a key river port and shipping center to all of Central Kentucky and as a chief stop on the old railway system. On the strength of this old economic base Augusta was able to draw other kinds of traffic that would be more attractive to a small boy.

As early as 1831 the famous London theatrical family of William Chapman(1) had emigrated to America and opened their "floating theater" which toured the Ohio River successfully and continued to prosper even after Chapman's death. Bryant's Showboat, also a family enterprise, gave its first performance in Augusta. The waterfront was papered with showbills announcing: "Bryant's Showboat presents *A Girl of the Underworld* with vaudeville between acts".(2) By the mid-1880's a youngster in Augusta might find entertainment by boarding the "New Sensation." The "Sensation" was owned by a Barnum-styled entrepreneur called Augustus French and his brightly colored barge theater featured comedy sketches, ventriloquism, and minstrel numbers. The minstrel show, which had become increasingly popular across the country, was a three-part performance, done in blackface with a few elements reminiscent of the vaudeville format. (Its problems and fictitious presentation of the black experience are the subjects of other works than this one, but for better or worse, minstrelsy was an important entertainment of the period and served to help create in great measure an "American" musical sound leading to the development of jazz.) These show boat entrepreneurs were "hands-on" visionaries, just the kind of producers that Walker admired and would emulate in later years. This kind of entertainment opened the world of public performance and its diversity of media to Stuart Walker. At the height of Augusta's commercial activity he could attend a stereopticon lecture or a chamber music concert or he could pay a small entrance fee to board a museum boat that presented history in the guise of spectacles.

There is nothing in the Walker family background that provides a reason for Stuart to be interested in the arts or in the theater. His father, Cliff, worked for the C.H. & D. Railroad when Stuart was small. His mother, Matilda Taliaferro Armstrong, was a hardworking housewife in accord with the Edwardian expectations of her generation. Nevertheless, his parents were not opposed to his interests and were, as far as we can tell, supportive of his youthful efforts to become schooled in a profession which must have seemed at best impractical and at worst immoral. Perhaps they sensed that he was from the beginning a loner who was not impressed by sports, who interacted with his peers only when he was in charge of an event or activity and who delighted in pretending for hours — satisfied with his own company.

When he was six years old, Walker contracted the measles, and his father gave him a toy theater complete with trap doors and two sets in the hope of making his son's convalescence more bearable. The toy was manufactured in Germany and the script (*The Bohemian Girl*) which came with it was written in German. His father re-wrote it and Stuart promptly mounted a production and sold tickets to his parents and any neighbors who were past the danger of contracting his childhood disease. Even at six years of age he was aware of the economic element essential to show business and apparently offered no complimentary tickets to his production. Long after he was over his bout with the measles he continued to present the same play until his audience rebelled and refused to attend again until there was a change of fare. At first he tried repainting the set and changing the title, but after his patrons discovered that it was the same script he knew that his only option was to write a new play. From then on he wrote one new play every week opening each on Monday night. It was a schedule that he would duplicate 30 years in the future when he operated his repertory companies in the Midwest. And it was not the last time he'd be associated with *The Bohemian Girl*.

As with many theatrical personalities, Walker's date of birth appears to be a moveable feast. As public figures grow older it simply becomes easier to gain employment and remain more attractive to fans if they stay as young as possible, and so it's no surprise that he endeavored to lose a few years along the way. Record-keeping did not need the public access or meticulous documentation that it is has come to demand in current times and finding a valid birth certificate has proven all but impossible. Although his birth has been listed as anywhere from 1880 to 1888, we can at least be certain of the day, March 4th. (3)

Actually, most information seems to point to 1880 as the most likely date even though it is at the earliest end of the speculative spectrum. So, he would have been just ten years old in 1890 when his family moved to Covington, Kentucky so that Stuart could attend school in Cincinnati, just across the river. Cliff and Matilda Walker must have had some indication of Stuart's unique ambition and curiosity to make that move. He remained in Covington for secondary school and during his senior year at Woodward High he won a medal for public speaking. In 1901 he moved to Ohio's major metropolitan area and entered the University of Cincinnati as an engineering student. A degree in theater was not an option at that time and though there is no documentation of Walker's activities in engineering he had some interest in the subject. In fact, his creative design abilities would eventually be at the forefront of his first theatrical success.

In college Walker was active in several clubs and suddenly discovered an interest in and a talent for his considerable social skills. He became a leader who apparently inspired both strong friendships and strong enmities, a trait that would remain with him during his lifetime. At this point the dichotomies of his personality were set: his stubborn ambition and his generous nature, his genteel persona and his temperamental outbursts, his sensitive ego and his sentimental loyalties all existed simultaneously and served to win supporters as well as to antagonize peers.

His activities in college were those with which he had experimented as a child and which would remain at the core of his work throughout his life: performing, directing, producing, and writing. The university newspaper and the yearbook show him to be an overachiever with a finger in any pie he could reach. The editorial comments in that yearbook are equally revealing. His biography in the annual publication reads:

Stuart Armstrong Walker - Sigma Chi and Sigma Sigma

I. Class President; Editorial Staff *McMicken Review*.
II. Staff *McMicken Review*
III. Junior Editor *Cincinnatian*, 1901; Forum; Stage Director Comedy Club.
IV. President and Stage Director Comedy Club; Forum; Editorial Staff *Cincinnatian*, 1903; University Club; Class Play. [personal quotation] "His beard, descending, swept his aged breast." [editorial comment] There are two ways of writing about Stu — the way his friends think and the way his enemies think... The mere fact that he has enemies shows that he amounts to more than those "nice fellows" whom everybody likes, and we only need add that, each in its way, the one class is as "wild" about him as the other.(4)

He was founder of the University's Comedy Club, and as a member of the Lead Pencil Club, wrote the script for his fraternity's dramatic entry in the School Carnival. The play *Hoop-La* was subtitled: *A Spasm in One Fit Concentrated by Stuart Walker*. Though not indicative of any future sophistication, the play does disclose a sense of humor and an ability to understand and a willingness to adapt to the audience of the day.

He was also active as a "chorister" in the Varsity Minstrels and had a keen interest in old English Ballads. Most of these ballads would have been originally performed unaccompanied and within a context of social conviviality, perhaps like the musical style at Augusta's black church. His ballad study would include liturgical and secular tunes, carols, madrigals, chant and polyphony.

Walker often credited George Miller (an instructor in the University of Cincinnati's English Department) with his introduction to the English Ballad and with offering the encouragement he needed. (5) These early musical interests were put to use at his theaters in underscoring the plays, lobby entertainment and most specifically in his development of the Jubilee Singers who would become part of the Cincinnati Company. Walker seems fortunate to have found in Miller encouragement and guidance in the cultivation of a profession for which his family could offer nothing more than moral support. In fact, with the exception of only one more major reference, his parents all but disappear from his public recognition of them.

With no official university program of study in drama outside the literary arena Walker sought out every opportunity to write or perform and tried out for the senior class play, *As You Like It*. He won the part of Orlando, a role he dusted off and used as his audition piece for acceptance into the American Academy of Dramatic Arts a few years later.

After receiving his B.A. degree from the University of Cincinnati some resources list him as working for the Southern Creosoting Company in Slidell, Louisiana and others place him in a nameless lumber camp. These are both possible since his father has been connected to both during this same time period. The work Stuart must have done for these companies cannot have afforded him the kind of creative outlet, leadership position, or intellectual insights that he had just discovered at the university.

It is certain that at some juncture after college graduation he contracted typhoid and was unable for some time to work or continue any kind of study. This had to have been frustrating and he was no longer able to even find solace in a toy theater. What the convalescence apparently did afford was the time he needed to make a life-changing decision — he would from then on find his solace in a real theater. This seems to be the first of many courageous acts of vision and self-reliance that Walker took on till the day he died. It is a quality that all successful theatrical professionals have in common. It is especially brave since Walker had no track-record or personal entrée into the theatrical world.

Walker moved to New York City and entered the American Academy of Dramatic Arts as a junior in 1908. His detour as a worker in Louisiana and his illness made him, at age 27, one of the older students in the program, but as is often the case, it also made him a student who knew what he wanted, why he was there, and very aware that he needed to catch up.

Walker found success with his college role of Orlando and so he chose a monologue from that play for his AADA preliminary audition. Toward the beginning of *As You Like It* Orlando confronts his older brother and asks to be recognized as a worthy equal. Orlando enters with his sword drawn and says:

> I am no villain. I am the youngest son of Sir
> Rowland de Boys. He was my father, and he is
> thrice a villain that says such a father begot
> villains. Wert thou not my brother, I would
> not take this hand from thy throat till this
> other had pulled out thy tongue for saying so.
> I will not till I please. You shall hear me.
> My father charged you in his will to give me
> good education. You have trained me like a
> peasant, obscuring and hiding from me all
> gentlemanlike qualities. The spirit of my father
> grows strong in me, and I will no longer endure
> it; therefore allow me such exercises as may
> become a gentleman, or give me the poor allottery
> my father left me by testament. With that I
> will go buy my fortunes.(6)

Shakespeare was, and still is, the benchmark for any serious actor and it is no surprise that Walker chose to use one of those remarkable roles for his audition. And the idea of Orlando fighting to go out into the world and find his fortune certainly resonated with Walker. The role of Orlando is that of a young man but its range (and type) is possibly more of a "leading man" than Stuart would ever be. Had he continued with a performance career (rather than going into producing and directing) he probably would have found his niche in character roles. Nevertheless he obviously did well enough to be admitted to the program. A copy of Walker's audition sheet was filed by Franklin Haven Sargent, founder of the Academy. Sargent opened the Lyceum Theatre School of Acting in 1884 after resigning from Harvard's faculty when the college rejected his proposal for a department of drama. The Lyceum was renamed American Academy around 1887 at the suggestion of Henry C. de Mille (Cecil B.'s father).

Additional audition information lists Walker as "six feet tall, 150 pounds, dark, and good looking." The preprinted audition sheet provides space on the right for the adjudicator's evaluation:

[typed form, transcription of #178/179,
handwritten records material includes all marking]

Personality	Good
Stage Presence	Good
Birthplace	Kentucky
General Education	University of Cincinnati
Previous Training	Something at college
Voice	Fairly good
Pronunciation	Good
Memory	Good
Reading	Fairly Good
Spontaneity	? (Health ?)

Distinction	fair (lacking vitality)
Pantomime	formal (much?)
Imitation	fair
Recitation	Orlando
Imagination	fairly good
	has sentiment
	a little tired
	danger of
	[indecipherable]
	lacks force
	comedy juvenile
	accepted April Junior (7)

The designation of "comedy juvenile" does seem to indicate that he was not a leading man type. Even at 27 he was very slender and perhaps still looked as though he was recovering from the long bout with typhoid. The comments "lacks force" and "lacking vitality" may also point to a period of lengthy convalescence or simply a lack of technique. He was still, after all, just an enthusiastic amateur. He most certainly was not lacking in charisma once he began advocating for survival of his companies. (All photos of him in later years show him in what could have been identical outfits no matter the passage of time and so, for his audition, he was probably dressed in his predictable tweed suit, bow tie and wearing glasses with round lenses.)

At that time the Academy was located in Carnegie Hall, in the tower on the east side of the building over the concert hall. The Junior course included "Physical Culture (Health, Fencing, Dancing), Voice, Stage Training (fundamentals of costume, makeup, stage business and stage mechanics), Pantomime, Life Study, Rehearsal, and Performance."(8) His second year was a busy schedule of rehearsal and public performance with occasional lectures and workshops. All in all it was a pretty comprehensive program.

His file card confirms that he was registered as a senior in 1909, but the name Stuart Walker does not appear in the graduating class of that year. The name "Marshall Stuart" does, and Marshall Stuart came from Covington, Kentucky, so it is probable that Walker was toying with the idea of a stage name while he was at the Academy. If that is correct, then Walker is credited with appearing in nine productions his senior year. Graduation was March 16, 1909 (a nice post-birthday present) and the commencement speaker was playwright Augustus Thomas. Thomas was in the vanguard of playwrights who were developing an American drama that strove to go beyond simple imitation or adaptation of European plays. He was known for his socioeconomic and political subjects as well as his treatment of American themes, characters and idiosyncrasies.(9)

Whether Walker graduated or not from the AADA, he was firmly committed to a professional track and wasted no time. He took a look at the Broadway scene and headed for the best. His ambition led him to seek employment and experience from the then current dean of Broadway producers and directors, David Belasco. Eight years before, Belasco had directed the United States premiere of Sophocles' *Electra* for the AADA, and the legend of Belasco's creative contributions to the Academy must have reinforced Walker's decision to seek him out. Having studied at the Academy would also have given Walker an entrée to meet the "Bishop of Broadway." The circle of the working theatrical professionals is small and, as in any business, a little name-dropping and/or some old-boy networking never hurts.

David Belasco was a vibrant, eccentric, and effective force in the American theater of the early 20th Century. He was called "Bishop of Broadway" because he always wore a jacket and collar that was reminiscent of a cleric's garb. He understood the value of a public image and used it to his greatest advantage. As both director and producer, he exercised total control over his company and his actors. His creative energy often spilled over into design and playwriting. He was an exponent of the popular stage who, while contributing greatly to realism in the areas of scenic and lighting effects, developed scripts which are best labeled as sophisticated melodramas. To some it seemed that Belasco misled the public into believing that he offered a new form of drama where there really was none. To others, including Constantine Stanislavski, he was performing significant work in dramatic technology. In any event, his success was enduring, his popular instincts unerring, and his passion for the theater unchallenged. Walker's early training and experience with Belasco were first-class. One very strong Belasco trait was his habit of taking an inexperienced talent and molding it from the ground up into a star performer. Walker too would always believe in the potential of young talent and in his own gift for sculpting those talents to fit his style. In an interview for the *New York Times* in 1932, Walker called Belasco "the wisest man of the theatre I ever knew."(10)

An influence that was more direct on Walker's ultimate goals and working patterns was Jessie Bonstelle. Much that "Bonnie" pioneered was later adapted and/or refined by Walker. Unlike Walker, Jessie Bonstelle was the fulfillment of her own mother's desire to go on the stage. Jessie toured as a "child reciter" and, while on the Stair-Havilland circuit, she made friends with E. D. Stair who later became owner of the Detroit Free Press and the Garrick Theatre, summer home of the Bonstelle company for many years.(11) Walker worked for Bonstelle in Detroit's Garrick theater and for her Buffalo company in 1914 and 1915. Bonstelle's first stock venture was backed by the Shuberts "who were anxious to create a chain of theaters as a move in their long war with Klaw and Erlanger."(12) In order to insure that their tours were booked, a few wise producers bought their own theaters and built their own touring empires across the country. In later years (and until the breakup of film studio monopolies) that would be the same way in which movie producers insured that their films would have an audience. Bonstelle worked for the Shuberts' legitimate theater chain.

She eventually directed stock companies in Buffalo, Ottawa, Toronto, Newfoundland, Halifax, Philadelphia, Providence, New York, and Northampton, Massachusetts before settling into her permanent home, The Detroit Civic Theatre, in 1925. The Shuberts offered no further financial support after their initial contribution, so her companies had to pay their own way. This is an enviable achievement. Her greatest success lay in the development of these solid, community-based, professionally-oriented companies.

One of Bonstelle's management strengths was her shrewdness in affiliating herself with all possible civic groups such as churches, schools, businesses, social services organizations, etc. Her instincts for audience development were keen and she apparently garnered backing from virtually all of Detroit. She kept a close watch on her patrons' tastes, even to the point of inserting ballots into programs and using their responses to formulate her next season's bill. Walker took this "family" approach with his audience and supplied his playbills with notes on coming attractions and filled his lobby with patron information and subscriber benefits.

The fact that Bonstelle was able to attain a permanent home for her company (which she also rented out) and to establish a venue for community entertainment, meant the fulfillment of a cherished dream. Walker trusted the counsel of mentors like Belasco and Bonstelle, and in a 1921 interview for the *Detroit Journal* he credited his success in Indianapolis entirely to Miss Bonstelle because "when I was facing financial disaster here just after my opening, she advised me to stick."(13) But he would not be able to match Bonstelle's success in terms of a permanent civic theater, and despite his other achievements, it was a failure he never forgot.

Margaret Storey, Bonstelle's stage manager, says it was at Bonnie's suggestion that Walker become an independent producer. When he did so it was by giving the media something so original that they couldn't help but support its invention out of sheer curiosity: the Portmanteau Theatre.

Chapter Two — The Theatre That Comes to You

A GOOD THEATER DESIGN IS VERSATILE, supportive, deceptively simple and friendly to the imagination. Possibly the best historical example of the perfect theater design is Shakespeare's Old Globe. It provided a variety of acting areas whose conventional usage was familiar to the audience and consequently needed only a few pieces of furniture to create an environment. Elizabethan playwrights trusted the audience to be imaginative collaborators and that's exactly the opportunity that Stuart Walker's design provided to his early audience.

That the architectural features of the Portmanteau Theatre resembled Walker's own childhood theater was no accident, but he enjoyed circulating a more lively scenario to explain the exact moment of invention. Walker always insisted that he was in a portable rubber bathtub when he realized that if someone could invent a collapsible tub, then Walker could create a portable theater. (It's hard to erase the image of Walker, dripping wet, still wearing his eyeglasses and bow tie, leaping out of the tub, like Archimedes discovering the principe of relative density, and running directly to the drawing board.)

Although the Portmanteau was the source for his early success it was meant ultimately only to be the core touring component for his dream. He believed he could eventually "promote a repertory system in six Midwestern cities which I hope will prove to be the seeds of a renaissance of American drama."(1) But first, he had to be a one-man-band as well as a designer, producer and director.

Walker found his first convert in Mrs. Coonley Ward, a society matron whom he met in 1914 when he was the guest speaker at a Drama League convention in Detroit. The League was a group of interested amateurs locally organized and loosely supervised by a national organization. They were active in supporting drama rather than creating it but their philosophy matched Walker's. On the front page of a Drama League program they announced: "The charm of these... theatres lies in their intimacy. The audience is not witnessing a spectacle which matches pennies with nature, but is treated to a phase of human nature transformed by the magic touch of the artist's hand and the poet's imagination."(2)

Walker's enthusiasm was so contagious that Mrs. Ward financed a Midwest speaking tour for him to gauge popular support and financial possibilities for his Portmanteau tour. He used as an example his earlier work in New York with children at the Christadora Settlement. The settlement house was one of several late 19th-Century philanthropic projects that built in a community and provided a place for social and recreational activities and learning. Walker came into the Christadora on the lower East Side of New York to provide and encourage theater for young audiences. He had become an excellent speaker and he must have been confident of financial endorsement because in the spring of 1915 he headed back to New York where he built his portable theater and hired an acting company.

Bathtub or not, his design was unique, practical, intimate, and most certainly portable. The proscenium measured 25 feet wide and 16 feet high with a playing depth of 18 feet. In fact, though it could be set up in most large meeting rooms, it was not prohibitively small. The design was remarkably compact so that when completely stowed, it fit into ten boxes and weighed only 3,000 pounds. There was a vast amount of publicity centering on the unique portable aspects of the design. The lighting setup consisted of four stand-lights each with one lamp of 250 watts behind which was a powerful mirror reflector.

Continuing with information from an issue of *Munsey's Magazine*:

> There are no footlights in the Portmanteau
> Theater...Mr. Walker has a system all his own.
> Its source is invisible to the audience, but
> the results are eminently satisfying.(3)

The first model of the theater was built by William J. Sheafe, Jr., and the theater's first scenic designers were Frank J. Zimmerer and Wilmot Heitland, both of whom remained with Walker for some time. The walls of the theater supported themselves by a system of interlocking and ground bracing.

Thanks to Constance D'Arcy Mackay's history of the American Little Theater Movement, we have an excellent description of the Portmanteau's decor:

> The stationary interior is four colors: black,
> blue, gold, and white....Half way up the
> walls is a wainscoting in black and above
> this black the walls are a deep, intense
> blue — the blue that is seen in the skies
> of Maxfield Parrish pictures. This blue
> is flecked with tiny disks of white and gold.
> There are three entrances. Doors at
> the extreme right and left facing each
> other, and made exactly alike, have
> curtains of blue. In the center back is
> a wide square arch, bordered in gold and
> black. The scene that is placed in this
> archway determines the whole atmosphere of
> whatever play is bring produced.(4)

What was intended to be the first public performance in a home base for the Portmanteau became only a set of "invited rehearsals" at that same Christadora Settlement house on July 14, 1915.(5) It was not until Valentine's Day in 1916 that the Portmanteau held its first paid performance in Boston. It's not surprising that any new venture takes longer than expected to get off the ground, so Walker didn't want to waste any more time and he started touring immediately after the Boston premiere and continued touring extensively even while developing his summer stock companies and producing on Broadway.

Walker instituted several policies to satisfy his personal production tastes when he founded the Portmanteau. The core of his acting company and technical crew, as well as his philosophies, all started with the Portmanteau. Paramount among his ideals was the value of retaining a permanent ensemble or repertory company which would be restricted neither by the constraints of the star system nor by strict adherence to lines of business. "Lines of business" was a term that described the type of character that an actor would play for a season or perhaps a lifetime. The most prevalent types/lines during this era were: leading man/woman, second man/woman, character, juvenile, injenue, and utility. (These types which are still present in almost every form of character-oriented performance trace their origins from ancient Roman Comedy through Commedia d'ell Arte and on into present-day television sit-coms. The foolish father, the clever underling, the young lovers are all part of this tradition.)

"Public attitude is changing," Walker said "and the successful company is one where the actor is versatile."(6) Though the following story is probably apocryphal it illustrates his enthusiasm for taking chances on young talent. It involved a New York manager who rushed up to him and asked where Walker had managed to get such a terrific cast of young actors. Walker turned to him and said "I got six of them from your company."(7)

Stanislavski and his troupe had recently come to the United States and made a terrific impression on all acting troupes. Walker joined in the chorus of those who praised the Moscow Art Players and said that the "apparent superiority of the Russians is due to their team work..."(8) The Moscow Art represented a set of players loyal to one director's vision; a company willing to share the spotlight; and, though we think of Stanislavski as producing mostly realistic drama, he too started out in producing fantasy like Materlinck's *Bluebird*.

Walker also wanted to prove that good theater could originate and thrive outside of Broadway and made a plea concerning "the dissemination of native theater...this American method of [Broadway] centralization is utterly destructive of the great things the stage has stood for in the past."(9) His criticism was that only the largest cities could hope to present the best dramatic material and that Broadway touring groups, when they came at all, only stopped in major metropolitan areas or were made up of very tired second-and third-rate casts. (None of this however stopped Walker from sending productions to Broadway when the opportunity presented itself.)

To use a young cast whenever the script allowed was a corollary of Walker's casting goals. "I think that a young player can be just as polished in his acting as one of more mature years," he said in a 1918 interview.(10)

Simplicity of design was a clearly expressed and often satisfied goal of the Portmanteau. Sets and props were limited, and Walker always invited the audience to collaborate in supplying the fuel for fantasy. It is interesting that, although he had no personal experience with Asian or African theatrical traditions, he was very interested in the same styles of performance that make up the basis for those ancient forms. This quote from one of Walker's early interviews has a great deal in common with the philosophies of contemporary director Julie Taymor whose *Lion King* makes a conscious use of age-old ritual theater:

> We know that religion started in wonder and mystery, the drama started likewise in wonder and mystery. This element is gone almost entirely. The performances of the Chinese theaters are the most eloquent realization of the old time theaters...After Shakespeare's day, as plays began to deteriorate, scenery began to improve."(11)

It's a sentiment that we often hear today when audience members at high-tech musical spectacles complain that they left the theater "humming the sets." Stuart Walker did not feel that his audiences needed helicopters or chandeliers to experience a catharsis. He topped off his philosophy with a phrase that illustrates equally his weakness for the sentimental. "People don't need scenery to see, and when I say 'see' I mean see with the most delicate eye, the soul."(12)

Another of the Portmanteau notions (probably inherited from Bonstelle) was doomed to decay once the realities of stock production set in. He started out with a commitment to financial independence. He wanted the Portmanteau to pay its own way. "If it cannot give an adequate return to playwrights, actors and designers, as well as to the director, something is radically wrong." he preached. "The public must support it."(13)

At first he was deservedly proud that, with the exception of one $3,000 loan, he was able to keep the Portmanteau tours going on what they earned at the box office. In later years he would have to recognize a different reality. But in 1916 the Portmanteau showed a profit of 20% on its initial investment.

Some of the credit for this success should go to the excellent management of Max Elser, Jr. and Russell Janney who worked at creating a profitable circuit of tour audiences. They took clubs, Drama

League centers, local groups, and colleges as a nucleus for a continuous tour.

A look at the Portmanteau's initial season discloses a venerable set of children's stage literature that, at the time, created an enviable output. It included: *A Fan and Two Candlesticks* by Mary MacMillan, *Gammer Gurton's Needle* by William Stevenson, *Crier by Night* by Gordon Bottomley, *The Gods of the Mountain, King Argimines and the Unknown Warrior, The Golden Doom*, all by Lord Dunsay; and *The Trimplet, Six Who Pass While the Lentils Boil, Lady of the Weeping Willow Tree* and an adaptation of Oscar Wilde's *Birthday of the Infanta*, all by Walker.

Intimacy and audience collaboration were a vital part of the Portmanteau's performance philosophy. Integral to this aspect of the performance was the thrust stage and the scripted appearances of non-plot characters called Memory, Prologue and the Device-Bearer. The Prologue acted as narrator and liaison with the audience and he often responded to questions (solicited or not) from youngsters in the house. The Device-Bearer functioned almost as an Oriental prop person, setting the few pieces of furniture or properties, but unlike his Japanese counterpart, he was costumed colorfully and not "invisible" in any sense. Memory set the event in motion by walking down the house aisle toward the stage and inviting "all you very grown-ups [who] once believed in all things true, to pass through there with me. I have something there that you think is lost....Come through the portals of once upon a time, but not so very long ago."(14) This establishes a very clear style of non-realism: breaking the fourth wall, addressing the audience and emphasizing the importance of their collaboration.

In addition to its novel design aspects, the Portmanteau was also attractive to a mainstream audience who were reluctant to embrace the new "realism" as personified by playwrights Ibsen and Strindberg. If audiences were looking for fantasy and romance, there was no better place to find it than in the Portmanteau repertoire.

Quickly becoming one of the most romantic figures of popular literature sold in America was Lord Dunsany, "an Irish Baron, a professional soldier, a Boar War veteran, a cricket player, a horseman, the best pistol shot in Ireland, and now the most interesting of all new poets."(15) Best known as a poet and fabulist, he also had a feeling for dramatic situation. His early plays were produced by the Irish Theatre. Genuine heroic feats in the war only added to his irresistible charm, and this preface to his collected works, written by Dunsany while he was on duty at the front, is a good sample of his stirring and emotional style:

> I do not know where I may be when this preface is read. As I write it in August, 1916, I am at the Eberington Barracks, Londonderry, recovering from a slight wound. But it does not really matter where I am, my dreams are here before you in the following pages, and writing in a day when life is cheap, dreams seem to me all the clearer the only things which survive. Now the civilization of Europe seems to have ceased and nothing seems to grow in her cornfields but death. Yet this is only for a while and dreams will come back again and bloom as of old, all the more radiantly for this terrible plowing, as the flowers will bloom again where the trenches are and the primroses shelter in the shell holes for many seasons when weeping liberty has come home to Flanders....Now I will not write further about

> our war, but I will offer you this book of
> dreams from Europe as one throws things of
> value if only to oneself at the last moment
> out of a burning house.(16)

The collaboration of Dunsany and Walker marked the happy encounter of two dreamers. This thread of romantic reverie which was the in-house style of the Portmanteau repertoire was far removed from the literature of the realistic movement and the daily news of the war which existed in a parallel universe. Dunsany's hope was "to make a work of art out of a simple theme and God knows we want works of art in this age of corrugated iron."(17)

Walker and Dunsany carried on a prolific correspondence before and during the initial productions of Dunsany's plays with the Portmanteau. In the last paragraph of a letter responding to Walker's request for the rights to *Golden Doom* Dunsany writes:

> ....though the world may be growing more
> barbarous in Flanders, what you tell me of
> your aspirations shows that elsewhere it is
> becoming more civilized. Matter of fact, it
> is not the ruins at Ypres or a street in Dublin
> that show the high-water mark of our times or
> barbarity. It is to be seen in London...in
> much of our architecture and in toys made
> for children.(18)

The two continued their correspondence, sharing philosophies and plans. For Dunsany, surrounded by the insanity of the trenches, it was surely a lifeline of hope as much as an opportunity for his plays to become known in America. For Walker it was a comrade in dreams, a fellow artist with whom to discuss the future of theatrical artistry as well as a protégé to present to American audiences.

When Walker sent the first set of designs to Dunsany he included this note:

> To my mind the play is the most important consideration....There is a story to tell and I try to tell it in the author's way....The scenery must never be obtrusive. It is not and cannot be an end in itself, but to me the lights come next to the actor in importance.(19)

Dunsany jubilantly agreed and then addressed his continuing discussion with Walker on the personality of the artist:

> An artist's message is from instinct to sympathy. I sometimes try to explain genius to people who mistrust or hate it and tell them that it is doing everything as a fish swims or as a swallow flies: perfectly, simply and with absolute ease. Genius is, in fact, an infinite capacity for NOT taking pains.(20)

Dunsany, like Walker, dealt in epic myth and ancient fantasy. They were best served by the milieu of the Portmanteau. Walker recreated a few plays from the Portmanteau rep for his stock companies, but they never worked as well outside that distinctive condition of the "theater that comes to you." This was partly because the Portmanteau's open design supported fantasy so well. But before long, even the Portmanteau had to succumb to an audience disillusioned by postwar reality. Additionally, one-act plays as an evening's bill were going out of style. It was due only to Walker's enterprising ambition and good fortune that he was able to cultivate as strong a company, as great a volume of good press, and as credible a reputation as he did before America lost its innocence. Moreover, in its present form the Portmanteau could not develop into Walker's ideal. He wanted each of six resident companies to prepare a repertoire of four plays. Each company would "stay at home a month, playing a different piece each week, then move to the next nearest city on the circuit. Thus each city would have a season of twenty-four different plays given under conditions that would make for smoothness and finish of performance."(21) Twenty-four plays a season is a tantalizing offer to any city.

Soon, as Walker started to move toward his larger goal, the press was taking a second look at the undeveloped potential of the Portmanteau. *Theater Arts Magazine* complained that the company could have made more artistic progress, and Boston's foremost critic (who in 1916 had named the Portmanteau one of the top 10 entertainments) said that "a little Portmanteau went a long way."(22)

But for the time being, the war was still raging and the United States finally entered the European "quarrel." Although not documented, we can assume that Walker's bout with typhoid (at about age 25) left him with a health deferment from active military service. Or he might have been past the age of conscription. Still, Walker and the theatrical community proved itself aware (in its own way) of the war. Broadway theaters often held competition benefits to see which production could contribute most to the war effort. Secretary of War Baker even appointed a military entertainment council. One money raising affair sponsored by the Stage Women's War Relief listed Walker's production of *Seventeen* as contributing $100 and placing second in donations only to *Cohan's Revue*. And in the provinces, there was a box-office war tax applied to all but the balcony and gallery seats. At the Cincinnati Grand, for example, a $2.00 box was levied $ .25; a

$1.50 box, $ .20 and the first three rows of the orchestra which went for $1.00 were charged $ .10.(23)

Walker was developing the Portmanteau's image during this first year of America's involvement in the war. The majority of scripts were either Walker originals or adaptations by Walker. *Six Who Pass While the Lentils Boil* was particularly popular and is still occasionally revived. *The Lady of the Weeping Willow Tree* reveals his fascination with the simplicity of Asian fantasy, and the inclusion of *Gammer Gerton's Needle* (a mid-16th Century secular prose farce) indicates a broad interest in the historical literature of the stage. The Portmanteau Plays were published in three volumes by Stewart Kidd Dramatic Publications and an advertisement described them as "more than a collection of highly diverting little plays, [it is] a record of an astonishing experiment in the American Theater."(24)

The Walker scripts are themselves more interesting in concept than in literary value. His dialogue is formal and slow-moving, but his plots and characters are imaginative and conceived with a high degree of visual beauty. At this point he was still basically targeting a young audience. "We are still children if we allow ourselves to remain in a youthful condition of thought," prompted Walker.(25) The majority of early press subscribed to this charming ideal.

Walker happily cut and pasted the growing number of positive reviews into his press books. Articles included praise such as: "more genuine beauty to the square inch than any fourteen-carat theatrical train that ever rolled into town"(26) or "a performance full of vibrance and charm, full of tang and novelty"(27) or "Stuart Walker took some of Pittsburgh's children on his knee yesterday afternoon (figuratively speaking) and told them the gorgeously illustrated stories that lie between the covers of the Portmanteau Theater story book just as fathers sometimes do."(28)

Once in a while a reviewer just couldn't appreciate the idea: "The worst harm it did was to make some people imagine that they had actually seen new art or stage theater production."(29) This was strangely reminiscent of the Belasco press complaint.

Every performer and company can point to a terrible review now and then and in the main, Walker's companies garnered good reviews wherever they went. Strangely enough as time went on, Walker seemed to become more and more sensitive to the few negative articles or to what he perceived as a lack of enthusiasm on the part of the press. From all that can be seen, the press was very aware of Walker and the quality of his work during his legitimate stage production years. Microfiche at the Cincinnati Historical Society, dozens of scrapbooks at the Lincoln Center Library, and several files at the Academy of Motion Picture Arts and Sciences in Beverly Hills make up only a small part of the press that Walker amassed during his lifetime.

The Portmanteau company worked very hard. A sampling of newspaper announcements from 1916 show the company touring to Brooklyn, Waterbury, Philadelphia, and Boston in February; Evanston, Baltimore, Wheeling, Ithaca, and Pittsburgh in March; St. Louis in April; Lexington and San Francisco in September; Troy (NY) in October; Hartford, Hanover, Poughkeepsie, Utica, Montclair, Manhattan, and Syracuse in November; and Rochester in December. It's exhausting just to read the list. These appearances were most often sponsored by a university or a drama group. Elser and Janney were doing their job.

Colorful brochures were just as effective in the early part of the 20th Century as they are in the early 21st Century. One attractive flyer that Elser and Janney produced read:

> Would you like to see...
> - a dramatic company completely composed of notable

>   players who really can act?
>   - plays with real throb and punch?
>   - costumes and scenery of original design and
>   such original staging as to have set a new
>   high standard for theater? (30)

Three more pages of the flyer feature quotes from contemporary reviews and several photos of the productions. It was a colorful, tight, clearly targeted advertising package that could work well today. Walker, doing his part, was speaking to as many organizations as possible. A political campaigner could not have stumped more.

Sometimes the press wasn't sure quite where to put the Portmanteau and it was (to some extent correctly) often placed with the Little Theatre Movement in America. The *Columbus Journal* tried to grapple with defining the new movement by saying: "Whatever you call them, you cannot ignore them for these experiments are bringing new life into the theater and we're feeling the beat of it way out here."(31) It's easy to see how many of the little theater notions fit the Portmanteau: anti-commericial, exponents of the rep system, centers of experimentation, intimacy between players and audience, and an ensemble spirit. *Theater Magazine* included some high profile independent theaters in their list of "Little Theaters." The articles mentioned the Portmanteau Players in the company of the Neighborhood Playhouse and the Provincetown Players.(32) Walker's reputation was in good company.

He continued to extend his company's reputation to the ultimate professional goal. An article in the *New York Times* of 1923 quips that, "Every now and then Stuart Walker puts a more or less timid foot in the direction of Times Square."(33) And this was true from the very beginning. There's a reason that New York has been called the "Big Apple" and songwriters Kander and Ebb articulated what all performers believe when they wrote "if you can make it there you'll make it anywhere."(34) So, as much as Walker protested that he could bring quality theater to any community, he couldn't resist the occasional siren call of the Great White Way.

He started early on experimenting with actually placing the Portmanteau stage on a permanent Broadway stage. In November of 1916, early in his Portmanteau history, he featured two weeks of matinees at the 39th Street Theater. In January of 1917 he played both matinee and evening performances for twelve weeks at the Princess Theater. He often used his own lighting system when playing the Portmanteau on Broadway. (This presented an interesting potential problem between the Broadway house technical operators and Walker's own designers and operators in terms of "turf". He must have come to some financial agreement that was acceptable to all sides.) He displayed a remarkable instinct that these plays needed to be presented in a reproduction of his intimate little theater or they would not translate or worse, lose their uniqueness. The Portmanteau Broadway engagements are not to be confused with later productions (such as *Seventeen*) which he brought into New York from his summer stock houses. The fact that he chose to put the Portmanteau on Broadway at all again demonstrates his reluctance to entirely disown the commercial theater.

At the height of Walker's reputation with the Portmanteau, E. H. Bierstadt (already a Walker cheerleader and official editor of the plays) heaped praise on the project by naming it the savior of the repertory system in a country

> strewn with the bleached bones of repertory movements which have died....It has remained for Stuart Walker, originator of the Portmanteau, to widen the scope of his work until it has included, as it does now, the most and indeed the only successful repertory company in America.(35)

Bierstadt could not have known that Walker was keenly aware of the Portmanteau's limitations, and was still looking for a better way to fulfill his original ambition.

Chapter Three — America's Best Plays, America's Best Actors

IN 1924, IN AN INTERVIEW CONSIDERABLY AFTER THE FACT, Walker said that "I had to give up the Portmanteau despite its popularity because it costs so much to travel."(1) Of course it's clear that Walker had long before set his sights on a permanent home base. The prototype was initially the Christadora House in New York City. Now he would look to the Midwest, nearer his roots, to set up a summer stock company of permanent actors whom he could use all year long in other ventures such as Broadway or touring. His ideal criteria remained much the same while he continued looking for "people who make public opinion in cities to organize [read finance] so that I can then exchange the units — not the scenery....Try, if possible, to have a young playwright attached to each unit and also lots of young actors."(2)

In 1916, just before his move to Indianapolis, Walker addressed this need for a company of young actors by inaugurating a training program for hopefuls who were without experience. (He consistently defended the value of early training and when, in 1931, he reluctantly gave up the Midwest venture, his first job in Hollywood was as acting coach to youthful contract players.) His student stage trainees (labeled disciples) attended rehearsals and performances and went into main stage shows when ready. Some sources say a fee was charged; others disagree or do not mention any financial arrangement. Walker himself loved talking about his apprentices and in 1930 in a letter he recalled that they "gave public performances for the subscribers. They played for me whenever I had a few minutes to spare, and then they got criticism from my viewpoint....Nearly all of them lived, breathed and ate theatre."(3) This doesn't seem to imply structured classes.

He later created more confusion as to the structure of apprenticeships by saying that he let young actors "hang around. If I gave one of them a part, I paid him. If I didn't, I didn't."(4) The average length of time for a disciple to become accepted as a full-fledged member of the company was usually three seasons. There was no mention of union membership going along with company membership but Actors Equity was very young and the complex qualifications, fees and contractual agreements which accompany today's entrance into Equity had probably not evolved by then. What is clear is that if any of those students were "star material" Walker would have put them in the permanent company without an apprenticeship.

Walker often said that anyone who spent at least two seasons with him was prepared for the competition. "My actors know how to take care of themselves...they keep themselves in fine physical trim, study voice, speech, pantomime, dancing, fencing, boxing and swimming." He asked them to "avoid too much liquor, get normal sleep and food."(5)

Walker was a director, producer, teacher, writer, and autonomous employer — all professions that allow a person to establish a strong emotional connection to collaborators and employees. He became their mentor, parent, father-confessor, advisor and controlling agent. He expected unquestioned loyalty from his company members.

Jon Jory (former Executive Producer, Actors Theatre of Louisville) and his sister, Jean Anderson, can recall lively discussions between their parents, Victor Jory and Jean Spurney, about Walker's group of apprentices. Victor Jory had a substantial track record before appearing with Walker, but Spurney's first professional job was with Walker in *Captain Kidd, Jr.* in both Cincinnati and Indiana. The Jory memories disclose an insider's perspective of the disciples since both Jory parents worked as full-fledged company members for Walker although at different times. Anderson recollects her mother referring to the apprentices as "acolytes, an entourage. There was a group of young men always sitting with him at rehearsal and trotting down the street behind him to the restaurant. You had to be 'in' with his entourage to spend any personal time with him."(6)

This kind of preferential treatment toward actors of either gender is, unfortunately, not unusual in the theater although some directors deal with favorites better than others. Additionally, the fact that Spurney expressly singles out only "young men" may or may not be an insight into Walker's personal life-style that has remained without public substantiation.

The most credible information on these student actors and actresses may be gleaned from a small collection of playbills housed in the Billy Rose Theatre Collection. The disciples did perform as a separate entity on occasion, and individuals were also asked to join the company from time to time. While acting as apprentices these students certainly did some go-fering and technical grunt-work, much as stock apprentices still do today. The disciples were a part of every company, starting with the first full summer season at the Murat in Indianapolis.

It would have made more sense for Walker to start in Cincinnati since it was his home, and he had already toured there in 1916. He told his press representative, Oliver Sayler, that he chose the Hoosier capital "because it was considered difficult."(7) A better explanation might be that he found a strong supporter in Ona B. Talbot. She was a forceful community figure who helped get business donations and sell tickets. She was the kind of figure who would not take "no" for an answer from any potential corporate donor. If a C.E.O. wouldn't see her at the moment, then she'd just sit in the lobby and wait until he did.

Walker opened in Indianapolis on May 14, 1917 at the Shubert-Murat, taking with him designer Frank Zimmerer (who stayed with him through the summer season of 1920) and a core of performers including Agnes Rogers, Gregory Kelly, Judith Lowry, George Gaul,

Beatrice Maude, and Lillian Ross. Like many New York actors, these are names that were well known and respected in the professional theatrical community on the East Coast. It's still true that many of America's most talented actors aren't known west of the Hudson unless or until they go into film or television. There are scores of other actors that worked with Walker who did become household names by the mid-century once they went to Hollywood.

His opening play was *It Pays to Advertise* and he immediately displayed that he understood the needs of his new position. He made the Murat more intimate by selling only 50% of the seating capacity, dividing the orchestra section in half with a latticework grill and giving the appearance that there was standing room only. He instituted a tradition of dancing in the lobby at intermission to a live band. And, in the style of the late Broadway showman David Merrick, he exhibited his understanding of publicity tie-ins which (when his petulance did not overwhelm his common sense) made him a master of community involvement. In this instance he took a cue from the *Pays to Advertise* title and invited local businessmen to put up a display in the lobby to "advertise" not only their particular product, but their personal support of his theatrical venture. Finally, he added a chamber ensemble which played sometimes pre-show, sometimes at intermission, and sometimes as underscoring. The trio of lady musicians was fortuitously represented by Ona B. Talbot. He soon discovered as do all novice producers that the musicians' union was a good deal more organized than the soon-to-become Actors' Equity Association. The musicians' union mandated that a minimum of five pieces must play in the pit of the Murat. That meant that a minimum of five players must be paid even if five weren't needed. Walker got around this by having the trio play in the house, the lobby, or the boxes — not in the pit.(8) The last member added to the Murat family was Marie Boicourt, who became Walker's secretary and remained with him for twenty-four years. What a source of history, color, texture, perception and stories Boicourt might have been, but when approached by a theater researcher in 1958 she was unwilling to comment on or share experiences from her years with Walker.

The most important production of the first Indianapolis season was the premiere of Booth Tarkington's *Seventeen*, and Walker eventually took the production to New York. It was a landmark in his career and, as he often did when he found a work which proved particularly successful, he gave it several incarnations, including a 1935 film version. The press (which, despite Walker's frequent complaints, was usually very good to the company) displayed excitement about the premiere and complimented the troupe for "substantial merit of the four productions already made and the increasingly enthusiastic public response."(9) Walker took a chance by extending the production for a second week, apparently a practice almost unknown in the city's stock history, and won full houses for the run.

Even though he was publicly committed to taking the resident cast to Broadway (he had often commented philosophically on the quality of his stock casts) he did replace the actress playing Lola Pratt with a very young Ruth Gordon when he moved the show to Chicago in preparation for the New York run. Gordon soon married fellow Walkerite, Gregory Kelly. She eventually enjoyed a long and successful film career and, after divorcing Kelly, married the successful script writer Garson Kanin.

The New York reviews were largely favorable and *Seventeen* played 100 performances at the Booth (a very respectable run at that time), an intimate house in New York and over 1,000 performances on tour.

But before any of this could happen the company had to finish its Indianapolis season. Walker, always ready to experiment with audience development, tried mounting two midweek matinees, probably aimed at courting the ladies and children who had made a shopping trip into the city. He used Wilde's *The Birthday of the Infanta* and *You Never Can Tell* as matinee attractions. Oscar Wilde's stories for children are beautifully crafted tales of redemption, loss, and love. They are a side of Wilde rarely seen and more than worthy of a second look. That the costumes for "Infanta" were based on the paintings of Velasquez illustrates the interest in style and research that Walker continued to lavish on his productions.

Walker wasn't alone in believing that there was a daytime audience out there. His competition included the latest installment of the *Pearl White* movie serial at a local film house. He also continued to revive Portmanteau successes within the season when he could arrange a double bill of one-acts. Toward the end of the first and relatively short thirteen-week season he produced Belasco's success *The Woman* (not to be confused with the Luce play, *The Women*), a script which would later become his first directorial project in Hollywood. His first season garnered praise from several corners and it's hard to imagine that the romance that had begun between Walker and the Hoosier public would ever end. Here is one example:

> It is more pleasing to be able to say on the eve of their departure that Indianapolis has shown a very marked appreciation of their efforts..."(10)

Just before the Walker company returned to Indianapolis in 1918 it made one of its six brief appearances in Cincinnati which were a prelude to settling there in 1922. Although Walker was hoping that Indianapolis would ask him to create a permanent year-round theater, he never stopped looking at other residencies as potential homes. Another stop before his return to the Indy Murat was Walker's next New York production, *The Book of Job*. *Job* remained another favorite of his which he produced in several cities. In a letter to his press agent, Oliver Sayler, he remembered with great pride that it was during *Job* he "used an individual spotlight method and that no other method had used it before."(11) Lighting design was always part of his vision as a director.

Job was not so much a play as a dramatization of a section of the Bible. Walker used the King James version (allowing only one alteration from the biblical text), staging it with two narrators, the biblical characters, a simple setting, and some innovative lighting. This style of presentation doesn't seem particularly unique to us now, but the production's impact would have been very extraordinary for Broadway fare: a team of narrators breaking the fourth wall; dialogue with a classical quality; a "unit" set that would serve to represent many locales. All of these elements continued in that Walker tradition that trusted in the ability of the audience to collaborate and believe within a style that was nonrealistic.

Even so, it seemed like a strange choice of productions to take to Broadway, but it did well as this overview of the season from the *New York Evening Post* reveals:

> It was Stuart Walker, perhaps who provided the richest store of varied and intellectual entertainment....The hearty appreciation with which his production of "The Book of Job," a work depending almost entirely upon the magnificence of its thought and splendor of expression, was received is infinitely significant.(12)

Another example of Walker's idiosyncratic sensitivity resulted from a patron's letter to an Indianapolis paper during the local production of *Job*. A Mr. Bates wrote suggesting improvements in script and staging.

Rather than ignore the note which was clearly written by an amateur, Walker proved himself remarkably thin-skinned for an arts manager and the incident sparked one of his many letter-writing frenzies. Throughout his career he almost always answered criticisms or perceived offenses with long letters defending his point of view and scolding the perpetrator of the comment. He wrote from his Carnegie Hall office:

> Mr. Bates seems to labor under the impression
> that I wrote the *Book of Job*....the authors,
> who are long dead, may not have know much about
> dramatic law but they knew how to say what they
> wanted to say. I found I could not improve on
> their work....Leave your tableaux for the
> strawberry festivals....Don't let us monkey with
> immortal things.(13)

By 1918 Walker needed to have a businesslike attitude toward turning out quality products on a weekly basis during long seasons which often included touring and special engagements like New York. He had his method of rehearsing down to a science. In 1920 he gave an extensive interview to the *Indianapolis News* which outlined his "theatrical laboratory."(14) This schedule saw few, if any, changes over the years.

First reading of a new play was at 10:00 each Tuesday morning in the rehearsal room in the northeastern corner of the foyer. Sitting around the table for the first reading of the new script the company shared coffee, tea, donuts, laughter, comments from Walker on his vision as director and from the actors who contributed ideas that might help to connect their performance to that vision. After lunch the cast took time to work on memorization. The company performed the old script that night (still working on the new one in the daytime) and also prepared for a regularly scheduled photo session of the current production after the Tuesday performance.

The company was able to complete blocking a three-act play on Wednesday morning before the regular Wednesday matinee and the next morning (Thursday) was given over either to a "walkthrough" to solidify blocking or to continue memorization before the regular Thursday matinee. The cast had all day Friday (till the evening performance) to run the new script and iron out any preproduction problems since Saturday morning provided the opportunity and challenge to work with props and some costumes as well as limited spacing on the stage without the set. The Sunday morning "turnover" of the set (striking the old show and setting up the new) gave the actors a morning off to sleep late, attend church, go over the script, do laundry, phone family. By Sunday evening (which was "dark") the cast was ready to run the show on the set. The last dress rehearsal took place on Monday afternoon just before opening night.

That the actors do not appear to have much free time is not only clear, but understandable. Even today, with what we imagine to be the protective aura of an actors' union, the summer stock schedule simply does not allow for the mutual existence of a full day off and a satisfactory opening in the same week. There was rarely a second thought to the priorities — it was all about the production. That same schedule put an equal, if different, burden on the nonperformance staff which included: J. K. Nicholas, press representative; Harold Holstein, business manager; Frank Zimmerer, scenic artist; Charley Reed, scenic artist; and a drop painter simply known as "Mose."(15)

Actors in the Walker company were paid not only for performance, but for rehearsal, which was generous considering that Equity did not require rehearsal payment until 1926 or even later under limited types of contracts. Walker was extremely proud and vocal about the respect with which he treated his actors. In a letter to Beulah Bondi (berating her for declining an offer) he stressed that the terms of her most recent engagement were more than usually generous as she had not "rehearsed unpaid during a period of four weeks and I did not lay you off, as I had every right to, between the stock production of the play and the regular road tour."(16) Walker demanded complete loyalty from his theatrical family and could not imagine any circumstances whereby an actor might need or want to accept an outside offer.

Although the union was not sufficiently organized to mandate much of what we now consider fair working conditions, actors were becoming aware of possible union advantages. George Gaul (playing at the Booth Theater in New York while on sabbatical from Walker) wrote in response to a newspaper letter attacking the creation of the actors' union on the grounds that it was a questionable activity:

> The conditions which prevailed in the theater before the association [Equity] must never return. If the Equity Shop is the only way of preserving the organization then we must have an Equity Shop. It is not un-American....We are all laborers. After playing the same role for 73 weeks I say that with conviction.(17)

Actors Equity, with its several regional offices, remains affiliated with the AFL-CIO and still sets contractual standards which include working conditions and payscale.

Much of Walker's summertime competition was Vaudeville and the variety acts which were still very much alive. In 1918 the English's Vaudeville House in downtown Indianapolis bill included: the acrobatic team of Mentalla and Didella; Down and Gomez with "songs quietly rendered"; Eldridge, Barlow and Eldridge performing a "rural skit"; Murphy and Kleine doing "diverting patter-and-song act"; and the

Radium Girls, "protected from the elements with a coating of bronze powder."(18) Although vaudeville's popular phenomenon wouldn't last many more years, it was a powerful entertainment force in its day. The genius of vaudeville was to please everyone. This approach enabled the vaudeville industry to create America's first mass audience. Vaudevillians had to lay the groundwork for a national audience who hopefully became more sophisticated as the acts became more refined.

Walker must have been holding his own against the popular competition because the Murat offered him a playing space during the winter of 1918, but he gratefully declined, citing other commitments, and said that he looked forward to returning the following summer. True, reviews during that May-August season had been erratic, but box office was good and that was the bottom line. *The Indianapolis Star* of August 11 summed up the impressive activities since the company's opening:

> Of those fifteen months, thirteen weeks for
> two successive seasons have been spent in
> Indianapolis, eleven weeks in Chicago, one week
> in Detroit, five weeks in Cincinnati, and there
> is a record for the run of *Seventeen* at the
> Booth Theater, New York of twenty-two weeks.(19)

The 1918 season closed with *Jonathan Makes a Wish* which reopened at the Princess Theater in New York less than a month later. This vehicle was an old Portmanteau script which was moderately received at the Murat and less well reviewed in New York. The consensus of New York's reaction to the Portmanteau method of presentation was that its novelty had worn off and it had become "an amateurish affectation."(20) That's what Lord Dunsany faced returning to an England and an audience that was greatly changed by the war. The world was being forced to grow up and the popular theater, which is more often than not a barometer of how we see ourselves, began to need escapist entertainment that was more sophisticated than the fare offered by Memory and the Device Bearer.

The Portmanteau was no longer a means to an end and would gradually be overtaken by the repertory companies that Walker envisioned. However dated it may have become it was a highlight of its era and created a well-deserved place in the development of American theater.

Walker returned to Indianapolis with renewed energy, and the prize of the 1919 season was an opulent production of *Kismet*. Local critics hailed it as "a personal triumph for [actor] George Gaul" and "a tribute to the ability of Mr. Walker as a director," and the community seemed proud that six members of the large cast had "served the Little Theater of Indianapolis in various capacities."(21)

As regards the wooing, there were now cities coming to Walker and asking for him to mount a trial season in their area. Louisville was among these, but Walker did not want to commit until a "subscribed season could be arranged guaranteeing $2,500 a week."(22) It was not until 1922 that the company played Louisville for three months. It is clear that in 1920 Walker still thought of Indianapolis as the spot from which he would operate his revolving repertory company. When the season opened with *Two Kisses* featuring Blanche Yurka and McKay Morris, Walker gave a brief speech after the final curtain referring to Indianapolis as his home and of his plans for the future. Blanche Yurka had been affiliated with Belasco when Walker was his manager and her substantial career weaves in and out of Walker's as do the careers of many high-profile names of the era who started out in his company. Yurka held him in high regard:

> I remember Mr. Walker's glee when in Cincinnati
> he could find standing room only in his theater.
> (Greater joy than this hath no manager!) It is
> a pity that this gifted and sensitive director
> should have been lost to the legitimate theater.
> The Midwest needed the kind of theatre which he
> provided and which he longed to make permanent.(23)

In one of those amazing life coincidences, Yurka's most successful career role was in a production of *The Bohemian Girl*, the play from Walker's childhood theater. Surely Walker was thrilled to present the real Bohemian Girl in his production.

Yurka was not the only professional who felt that Walker was especially talented. "Directing theory was in short supply during that period" stresses Jon Jory, "mostly traffic control, louder, faster. My parents [Victor Jory and Jean Spurney] always said that Stuart Walker was better than most."(24) Anderson agrees that her mother was "delighted to get into the company because [Walker] was always busy and ambitious."(25)

There began about this time in Indianapolis a subtle stirring from the theatergoing public which, if reflected correctly in the press, seemed to require something from the Walker company which was implied, but never articulated satisfactorily in print. Although the end of the 1920 season showed box office improvement, the local press was bemoaning the lightweight choices which made up the season. And facing Walker when he returned in 1921 was competition from an unlikely source: Gregory Kelly and Ruth Gordon, former members of his company, had decided to open a summer stock house of their own at English's Theater. Gordon had been with Walker since she played Lola Pratt in his Broadway production of *Seventeen*. He must have felt some sense of betrayal even though he could intellectually sympathize with their ambitions. As it turned out, the Kelly/Gordon venture lasted only one summer, but there remained an underlying discomfort that permeated the whole situation and some wrangling in print over just whose company came out on top that year.

Walker pulled out his big guns in 1921 with a production of Maeterlinck's *Monna Vanna*, a vehicle for Blanche Yurka as well as the enduring and popular *Smilin' Through* with Elizabeth Patterson and George Gaul. He revived *The Book of Job* in a special series of matinees under the sponsorship of the League of Women voters, and an unusual offering during the season was *Come Seven*, a play by Octavius Roy Cohen that featured the entire cast in blackface. Although not a minstrel show, the tradition of blackface was obviously a comfortable enough convention that a legitimate "book" plot could be built around it. Blackface performance was, in fact, still occasionally seen in film and on stage as late as the 1950's.

In the same season Walker also presented a premiere dramatization in Indianapolis and New York of *Main Street* based on the novel by Sinclair Lewis. Neither Indianapolis nor New York were particularly appreciative of the privilege.

The high point of the 1922 season was *The School for Scandal* with Spring Byington as Lady Teazle. Spring Byington was to become successful in early television as the title character in "December Bride." *Scandal* is a Restoration script full of fun and style which would create good box office response in a season like Walker's. Photos of the costumes by Grace Latimer and the sets by Almarin Gowing reveal a production that was expensive but not inventive.

Newspaper commentary was very good but also seemed to serve notice that this production norm was becoming the exception:

> It is likely that many local playgoers will wonder why Mr. Walker cannot keep up to the standard of the *School for Scandal*, but it would be too much to expect of any producer in repertory to do so well week after week.(26)

It would appear that Walker was in competition with himself.

Earlier in August of 1921 the *Indianapolis Star* reported "a slump which holds the theaters and the movies in many cities",(27) but the Walker season did not begin to reflect a general decline till 1922 when a *Star* reviewer noted that patronage was not up to normal. That same article, however, found fault with the public rather than the company since "the productions give evidence of the meticulous attention Mr. Walker pays to every detail."(28) This seems to contradict the previous comment pointing to an uneven standard of quality.

The level of stress had to be considerable. Walker had created a complex machine accountable to his public, accountable to his company, accountable to his dream. In addition to the struggling 1922 Indianapolis season, Walker produced his first official Cincinnati summer and a short season of November to January in Louisville. He showed the strain in a classic Walker backlash reported in *Variety* when he "voiced his grievance before the Altrusa club when he called the Indianapolis people provincial. Walker did not state how long it was after he got here before finding that out."(29) Even though the New York paper deals good-naturedly with the outburst, it is doubtful that the theatergoing public of Indianapolis found it quite as amusing.

In 1923 the company kicked off its seventh season in Indianapolis, marking its 93rd week of production in that city. Walker opened with two good scripts: *The Girl of the Golden West,* featuring Yurka (a Belasco creation later to find a lasting place in the opera world), and *Peter Ibbetson* with Morris. Walker and his staff gave a great deal of attention to the production values of these two openers. Reviews were excellent and photographs of both sets indicate provocative designs. McKay Morris, who had been away from the company for two years acquitting himself favorably in New York, "achieved last night the greatest triumph of his career with the Stuart Walker organization."(30) But for some reason even these properties of high production value did not shore up attendance or insure the press coverage to which the company was accustomed. In September of 1923 the *Star* ran a review of the season expressing "serious doubts as to whether Mr. Walker would return next year....Theatrical superstition dictates that a stock company can not continue for more than seven years in one place."(31)

Superstition had little to do with it. Both George Gaul and McKay Morris, who were extremely popular members of the company, had been absent and working in New York for several seasons. The Cincinnati company also took a few favorites, such as Elizabeth Patterson and Beulah Bondi (who joined the Murat company in 1919), away from the patrons who felt a proprietary right to them, and it became evident that Cincinnati was already treating Walker with the enthusiasm he felt the company deserved. The support of ex-Governor James Cox for Walker's Dayton company at the Victoria Theatre proved to be influential in the formation of the Cincinnati group. Walker felt betrayed by the Hoosier experience, and "the always sensitive Walker saw attendance dip and criticized the press for lack of support."(32) In a letter to *Indianapolis Star* critic Robert Tucker he remarked that "when a city fails to support even adequately the plays and the actors I gave them the past summer, every manager in the country must hesitate before he risks his money in that city."(33)

The company did not, however, slow down in the fall nor in the year to come. They previewed *Time* in Indianapolis before taking it to New York, and the Portmanteau toured its last season and took *Job* on the road along with the plays of Dunsany and Walker. This was in addition to Walker's regular Cincinnati season and the inauguration of a Dayton engagement.

Walker returned to Indianapolis to play in B.F. Keith's theater during the summers of 1926-1928, but he never seemed to feel comfortable in Keith's, and in 1928 the *Times* released an interview with Walker who adamantly refused "to cut our product." The newspapers and the public in Indianapolis seem to be in no mood to "accept us at face value."(34) The volume of Hickman and Tucker reviews shows them to have been genuine supporters of the Walker company, and the press welcomed him back, affirming that Walker had given them "many, many productions ranking with the very best in the country".(35) So although these journalists agreed that Walker had not received "the box office patronage he deserved" they also felt that Walker behaved badly by blaming them when they had in fact endorsed him throughout. They were right. In frustration Tucker complained that "there is a limit to the use of superlatives in any newspaper office — which numerous theatrical people seem not to understand."(36)

Harsh words notwithstanding, the Walker company contributed greatly to the cultural climate of Indianapolis in the 1920's and to the development of several talents who had long careers on the stage or in film. In 1936 Elizabeth Patterson spoke to *Star* columnist Patrick Corbin about the stock days, reminiscing that "...many a time as I sit on some dimly lighted set in a studio in Hollywood, I think of the Stuart Walker days in Indianapolis, wishing they might come again."(37)

The year 1926 marked two very personal events in Walker's life. His mother died at the Vernon Manor in Cincinnati and shortly afterward Walker formally adopted a young man with whom he had formed a close friendship. Arthur Helm was in his teens when he was introduced to Stuart by an aunt who had known the Walker family in their Augusta, Kentucky days. She took Arthur to see a Murat production and he accompanied her backstage after the performance. (At the time of his adoption Arthur was 19 and his natural parents and two siblings were alive and living in Indianapolis.) There is little written about the relationship and Arthur is mentioned publically primarily in Walker's obituaries. If there was a relationship that went beyond that of father and son it was carried on in a most discreet manner. Arthur was in attendance at his adopted father's deathbed and he inherited all of Walker's property in Beverly Hills, New York and Louisiana. In 1958 Arthur Helm Walker was living in Mexico and inquiries made to his last known address have gone unanswered.

The old Walker home is located at 321 Riverside Drive. It is only a few steps to the Ohio River from the front yard. In pre-Civil War days the River provided a route to freedom from Kentucky to Ohio.

This is the view that Stuart Walker the child would have seen from his door. The Augusta Ferry is one of only two currently operating on the Ohio River.

Now closed and boarded up, the old Methodist Church still stands in Augusta, Kentucky.

The Taft Theater, downtown Cincinnati. Walker's newly incorporated company played its last season here.

A studio proof of Stuart Walker (for once without his bow tie) taken during the years when his Portmanteau Theater was flourishing. Courtesy of Billy Rose Theatre Division, The New York Public Library for the Performing Arts, Astor, Lenox and Tildon Foundations.

An opulent production of *Kismet* at Walker's Indiana Murat Theatre Series. Courtesy of the Billy Rose Theatre Division, The New York Public Library for the Performing Arts, Astor, Lenox and Tildon Foundations.

Stuart Walker and Booth Tarkington discussing Walker's successful adaptation of *Seventeen*. Courtesy of Billy Rose Theatre Division, The New York Public Library for the Performing Arts, Astor, Lenox and Tildon Foundations.

One of Walker's early role-models was David Belasco, the "Bishop of Broadway," whose *Girl of the Golden West* became a vehicle for Blanche Yurka when she played it many years later for Stuart Walker's repertory company. Courtesy of the Cincinnati Museum Center—Cincinnati Historical Society Library.

Anna Sinton Taft, half-sister-in-law to the President, was patron of the Cincinnati Walker Company and almost single-handedly financed it between the Stock Market Crash and her own death in 1931 when it could no longer operate financially. The Cincinnati Tafts were supporters of the Arts on many levels and their own stunning collection of paintings is currently housed in the Taft Museum, Cincinnati. Courtesy of the Cincinnati Museum Center—Cincinnati Historical Society Library.

Chapter Four — The Stock Tradition

INDIANAPOLIS WAS THE BEGINNING. Cincinnati would mark the end. But before reflecting on those last Ohio seasons where Walker came so close to realizing his goal, it is important to recognize that intertwined and overlapping in the same time frame were the successful residencies of Walker companies in several Midwestern cities. These companies were the sort of tentacles he had always envisioned as reaching out from the parent base. And if the parent changed once in a while, that didn't seem to affect the system. There were often as many as three companies performing simultaneously among Indianapolis, Cincinnati, Louisville, Huntington, Parkersburg, Dayton, Detroit, Cleveland, Wilmington, and Baltimore.

It is also important to consider the nature of the stock experience which formed the core of Walker's endeavor and which was a way of life to a generation of actors. The undertaking of one-week stock for year upon year is in itself a feat of daring and a praiseworthy accomplishment. Although "statistics may not be considered a proper subject for comment in a column devoted to artistic enterprise," wrote William Goldenburg, "the statistics pertaining to the Stuart Walker Players in Cincinnati form an eloquent tribute to the achievements of the popular local dramatic producer and his faithful coworkers."(1) This was the same year (1926) that Walker gave Indianapolis audiences another try for fifteen weeks and Dayton for eight. Walker entrusted Indianapolis to George Somnes and Dayton to Alexander Dean. Just as Belasco and Bonstelle had charged Walker to manage their auxiliary companies. Somnes had already distinguished himself by being the first American to gain distinction with London's Old Vic and was a popular figure in the Walker organization. Walker, meanwhile, took over direction of the Cincinnati group and, when available, inaugurated any new residency himself. What an era of excitement, pressure, exposure, and power for this country boy who gambled it all and looked as though he might win.

In its hey-day one-week stock companies were highly successful institutions and were vital to the growth of a popular theater in America. It hadn't taken long for all Americans to move from attending live theater at least once a week to going to the "picture-show" at least once a week. Outside of New York, Chicago and possibly San Francisco, legitimate theater attendance was dropping. Walker wanted to present productions that would lure people back to a form of entertainment that cost more than film and that also demanded a commitment of collaboration from its audience. It remains a hope of every artist that if the product is good enough, it can compete for an audience.

These productions provided an opportunity and a challenge to the actor which cannot be duplicated today. "The actress who has in three seasons played 100 parts is surely better qualified than the actress who has in the same length of time played possibly five,"(2) offered Bonstelle in 1905. The responsibility of memorizing 25 to 40 roles a season was staggering. According to Jory, his parents would take turns staying up all night to learn their lines. Jory's father, Victor (whose most visible roles were probably Helen Keller's father in *The Miracle Worker* and the overseer at Tara in *Gone With the Wind* was one of the many actors who worked with a Walker company. "They didn't think anything of it," he said; "you couldn't find an actor today who wouldn't quail at the prospect."(3)

The actors worked only with sides, and few people had access to the entire script. Their first exposure to the entire play would be that Tuesday morning read-through. Sides contained only the actors' lines with four or five words of the preceding speech. They were typed into a small booklet about seven inches wide and five inches high. These sides were returned to the rental house and each actor was responsible for erasing all changes and blocking that he/she had entered (in pencil, of course).

Playing so many roles, some of whose substance was less than classic, meant that versatility was a primary virtue. Due to the limitations of time, the emphasis was necessarily upon the play as a whole. Any stock director had enough on his hands to instill some measure of freshness, style or vision in a piece without having much time to coach the individual actor. That is why a resident company of actors would be a great advantage. They were used to working together, knew what to expect from each other and from the director and had developed a working relationship that included some form of professional ESP.

The actors were often hard-pressed to provide themselves with a new characterization. Jory offers this greenroom dialogue the likes of which his father said took place before many first readings:

> "Well, Vic, what are you doing this week?"
> "Thought I'd wear an eye patch."
> "You can't do that, my role has to have one next week."
> "O.K., then I'll do the Irish accent."(4)

Jory adds that "a generation of brilliant actors came out of this [stock] tradition. It was a valid training ground and we'll never find out how it works....It came along just after touring and before film and it can't happen any more."

Probably the closest we can come to examining the tradition and success of this training is to look at the incredible generation of actors that came out of England who learned their craft in the "provinces" and worked their way up to leading roles. This kind of training provided a chance to watch the best, a chance to fail outside of the spotlight, a chance to stretch outside of type, a chance to recognize the value of a small role, a chance to work in less-than-perfect scripts as well as a chance to work on marvelous classics.

There were a few other organizations whose development at this time is worth a brief comparison. In doing so, we can also see the shift Walker's company had taken since "abandoning" the Portmanteau ideal. The common perspective of these groups was that the centralization of theater within the Broadway district was detrimental to creative growth. New theatrical movements developed "more or less in explicit opposition to the taste, the standards and the working conditions of the entertainment industry."(5) Different types of "anti-broadway" theaters evolved from a common view. Although, as we've seen, many of these producers weren't above mounting a production on Broadway.

The early Portmanteau, for example, bore a resemblance to the independent little theaters who professed an opposition to commercialism. On the other hand, a stock company must develop some commercial potential to exist; so the subsequent Walker organization fulfilled Sheldon Cheney's belief that

> the real art of the theater in America depends
> for its fullest development upon the emergence
> of fixed local playhouses with resident companies,
> dedicated to repertory production...directed by
> artists rather than businessmen... (6)

These institutions should, in Cheney's view, serve a community in relation to theater as the art gallery serves it in relation to painting and sculpture. The following contemporary companies had no equivalent to the Walker touring component and none should be confused with the "civic" theater whose definition demands community participation on stage as a major criterion.

The Detroit Civic bore the closest resemblance to Walker's company. Bonstelle began, as noted earlier, by directing stock in several cities and finally settled into the Garrick with a great deal of support from the Detroit community. Bonstelle rehearsal schedules as described in Margaret Storey's "Players Nursery" are very similar to those already described by Walker. This is simply because it was the only possible way to crank out a show a week with some integrity. Both Bonstelle and Walker developed a reputation as "star makers," and a list of actors who worked with Walker includes Spencer Tracy, Basil Rathbone, Anne Revere, Shirley Booth, Peggy Wood, and Will Geer among others.

Another contemporary, The Hedgerow Theatre, founded in 1923 by Jasper Deeter, was conceived as an "independent, non-subsidized, nonprofit" theater and could be considered as semiprofessional in comparison to Walker's professional setup. The Hedgerow (located in Rose Valley, Pennsylvania) produced a genuine repertory schedule and was never an Equity house. This meant they never had to comply with the requirements or working conditions set by the union nor did they have to meet a minimum pay scale. Walker, whose stock company after 1919 would be operating during the early stages of Equity, might not have been burdened with compliance to as many policies as are now mandated by the union, but a majority of his actors had a long-standing history in the commercial theater and would have required handling with comparable professional courtesy and political sensitivity. (Walker was himself a lifetime member of Equity.)

The Pasadena Playhouse invites comparison only at the beginning of its development. It was founded by Gilmor Brown, another strong and independent manager who, in the early days, appeared (as did Walker) in the productions. By 1930 however, the Pasadena Playhouse had taken on a high profile due to the number of film names who either appeared as cast members or attended the productions. The aura of the place became one of potential "discovery" for every young film hopeful, and that unique position in the film community immunized it from many of the conventional stock problems. The support it received from Pasadena in obtaining a permanent facility is reflective of the "family" support gained by Bonstelle and sought by Walker. It must have been "a closed shop" for creative personnel because it seems reasonable that Walker would have otherwise sought the occasional directing project there once he moved to Hollywood.

Common to these companies was the eventual dependence on subscriptions for pubic relations as well as for cash flow. A company's "subscribing audience always feels a proprietary interest and it [the subscription system] is the link between the producing group and the community."(7) The *New York Tribune* took notice that "business methods are encouraged by the subscription plan. In Cincinnati Stuart Walker operates a subscription play ..."(8)

The variety of titles offered to subscribers during the typical Walker season seems to reveal no company identity nor any indication of local taste. At first glance, one might be inclined to point to bad programming as part of the reason for the Indiana slump. But looking at seasons of comparable presenters, it's reasonable to assume that the broad-stroke style of presentation was part of the standard box office appeal and that the reasons for patron decline at the Murat cannot be that easily determined.(9) Confident of acceptance in Cincinnati, and fully committed to the stock tradition, Walker wrote off the indifference of Hoosier audiences and put his energies to the opening at the Cox in Cinncinati.

Chapter Five — Almost Home

THE COMPANY WAS GETTING PRESS in the Cincinnati area as early at 1918 and was considered "unique in that it has no leading man and no leading lady, for Stuart Walker believes that his company would be a democracy in which members have definite and arbitrary places."(1) These tours played at the Lyric Theater but the *Tribune* noted in May of 1918 that in spite of good notices, support had not been good. The article speculates that perhaps the four weeks of experimentation had come too close to the end of the regular season. How torturous and often pointless it is to try and pinpoint why a critically acclaimed season did not do as well at the box office. But it's easy to imagine several discussions given over to publicity failures, to season selection, to subscription development — and none of them substantially at fault.

Even so Walker returned for the next four years until the company was an accepted fact, a theatrical institution and Cincinnati was, at last, ready to welcome him on a permanent basis. He opened on April 24, 1922 (a little over a week before the Indianapolis opening), presenting *Honors Are Even* with a new lighting system at the Cox Theatre, a proscenium arch stage. (A proscenium house is the structural style of theater architecture with which we are most familiar. It separates the performer from the audience by a frame which symbolizes an invisible "fourth wall" through which the audience views the action on stage.)

The company played four seasons at the Cox, two at the Grand Opera House and its last five seasons at the newly-opened Taft Theater. Seating capacity for the Cox was 1,465, for the Grand, 1,600 and for the Taft, a challenging 3,600.(2) Remember that none of Walker's actors had the benefit of amplification and so they relied on the old-fashioned training that allowed for a healthily produced vocal power that filled a large house for eight shows a week. Walker continued to pledge his energies to Cincinnati and promised to build his sets in town using local materials as much as possible. He emphasized his student days at the University and said it had always been his ambition "to establish a high class production theater company for his people."(3) It must have been a moment of real pride to open his season in his university town and within an hour's drive of his birthplace.

In 1923 Walker was still playing in Indianapolis, and juggling actors' schedules was harder than ever. This became particularly evident when George Gaul refused a thankless role in *Our Little Wife* at the Murat. Johnny Wray, who was then playing in *Come Seven* in Cincinnati, took over the role and had to commute daily between the two cities while *Wife* was in rehearsal. Spring Byington also had to commute during rehearsals for *The Boomerang*. This would have been close to a three hour commute each way — an exhausting trip especially as the run went on.

In spite of problems, the Cincinnati season continued to grow with popular attractions such as Blanche Yurka in *Girl of the Golden West*. On a quick trip through town, J. J. Shubert said that "the success of the Stuart Walker Company at the Cox is one of the indications I've had that the day of the stock company is coming back."(4) Walker branched out into projects such as the production of *She Stoops to Conquer* on radio station WLW and presented an extended schedule of "disciple" matinees. He also launched the Jubilee Singers who not only performed at intermission but also did a stint on the radio. As always, Walker reached out to as many entertainment media as possible. The Jubilee Singers were made up of the younger members of the company and specialized in gospel music. They also served as ambassadors of goodwill at functions such as the Chamber of Commerce meetings where they offered a program of spirituals. There is no mention of a vocal coach or arranger for the group, but it seems likely that Walker was instrumental in choosing their style of music. He had, after all, been exposed to Stephen Foster's songs as well as to the local gospel choirs in Augusta and felt a familiarity with the style.

He next became active as an advisor on the board of Clare Tree Major's experimental drama school in New York City where children up through high school who wanted to learn professional stagecraft participated in classes and productions. Film greats George Arliss and Jane Cowl were also on the board. Toward the end of the 1923 season, Walker mounted another New York-bound play called *Time*. The Cincinnati press was enthusiastic, calling the cast unusually strong. New York was not so taken and the kindest review termed it "a sweet gentle sort of thing, but thin."(5) In some ways Walker was using the Midwest as a sort-of "Off-Broadway" tryout for new works in the same way that Des McNauff uses the La Jolla Playhouse for new work development or the Goodspeed Opera House in East Hadem tries out major revivals for a Broadway track.

Time was still running in January of 1924 and its Broadway competition included: *The Ziegfeld Follies, The Swan, Seventh Heaven, Abie's Irish Rose, Rain, Aren't We All, Artists and Models, The Greenwich Village Follies, Music Box Revue, One Kiss, Laugh Clown Laugh, Cyrano de Bergerac, The Bluebird, St. Joan* and *Kid Boots*. It was not a season for "thin" fare.

Walker's gifts in the area of public relations had a chance to flourish in the warmth of a stable environment. Although he was hardly as hardcore as showman/producer David Merrick, he still experienced a similar streak of delight when finding an "angle" or getting free advertising space. He arranged with the newspaper to give away a set of tickets for each show, drawing from names of the readers who purchased want ads. (Classified buyers got a bonus and Walker got free advertising). He "volunteered" a group of young women in his company as hostesses for an afternoon of service at a city-sponsored benefit sale. He bought a "wireless" radio set for the green room and released photos of his actors listening on the headsets between scenes. Whether he was persuading a corset shop manager into advertising *Madame X* models during the play of that same name, or collaborating with a local clothing store to sell all its merchandise for $17.00 during *Seventeen*, Walker never missed a chance to position his company name in the public eye.

Walker was also working hard to create a continuity. The company did not even take a break during the 1924-25 Cincinnati schedule, working for seventy weeks straight — that's worth saying again: seventy weeks straight! To ensure the continued quality of this strenuous, multi-season venture, Walker continued to rely on the talents, loyalties and popular standing of McKay Morris, Judith Lowry, Ann David, Donald Macdonald, and Beulah Bondi. The season included a revival of *Main Street*. The production fared much better in Cincinnati than it had earlier in New York where criticism was mainly focused on a poor set design and the choice of vehicle. But even Broadway critics had been admiring of the second act and the performance which revealed a "masterly depicted 'slice of life'." (6) Support for the company was strong and building. The momentum of the 70-week blitz season carried into sales for the next summer. Goldenburg, the *Enquirer* (7) columnist who followed the company's progress carefully in Cincinnati, expressed in 1926 his support for what he felt were two of its strengths: the great number of actors and the high average of new plays Walker introduced through the company each year. Walker offered a rare guest appearance to an actor outside of the company by inviting Basil Rathbone (who would become the Sherlock Homles of the Hollywood '40's) to appear in *Love is Like That* in August of 1926. The same year saw Peggy Wood in the title role of Shaw's *Candida*, and Walker himself appeared in the season's closer, *Begger on Horseback*. *Candida* and *Begger* were both popular works.

There was a solitary article in the *Cincinnati Commercial Tribune* at the end of the 1926 season which implied that Walker had settled on a four-city circuit to begin in 1927 which would not include Cincinnati.(8) This plan did not result in anything and the next Cincinnati summer season took place as if nothing had been said.

By 1927 a few of Walker's faithfuls had begun taking brief sabbaticals to play in films. Elizabeth Patterson compares the experience of working in each medium at a time when films were silent and, as far as anyone in the business was concerned, likely to remain so. (*The Jazz Singer* was right around the corner to prove them all wrong.) "On stage," she explained, "the actor does not have to rely on pantomime alone to convey personality to the audience...he is also facing an audience of sympathetic human beings and not the merciless eye of the camera." Later in the same interview, Patterson compliments Walker's directorial abilities, saying that, unlike film directors, Walker "tells his players what to think, not what to do. He has enough confidence in the ability of his players to know that they understand the meaning of the lines."(9) This kind of comment is strong praise for Walker's ability as a coach as well as his ability to coordinate as a director. It is a rare combination.

Legitimate entertainment venues were doing well in 1928 Cincinnati. The facts flew in the face of the old belief that "Cinti is not a show town"(10) as Goldenburg proudy noted in his column announcing that Ziegfeld's *Rio Rita* opened at the newly renovated Erlanger Grand Opera House, that the National Players were at the Cox, and that the Walker company was contracted to play through the winter at the Taft. This relative security meant that Walker could indulge a favorite enterprise and produce some theater for young audiences. In December he gave a special matinee of *Mrs. Wiggs of the*

Cabbage Patch for 1,500 school children. The next week he revived *Six Who Pass While the Lentils Boil* and *Sir David Wears a Crown* for another children's performance. His mantra was: "If the theatre must have a future then it must have an audience."(11) And those children must have been that future. He then proceeded to mount a sizable production of *Treasure Island*.

During this period of growth the press was supportive in giving preproduction coverage and the majority of reviews were excellent. Resident actors continued to become the "property" of subscribers, and citizens who had never been down the aisle of any theater were adding the Walker company to their list of "must see" metropolitan attractions. Walker was getting good notices from everywhere: "Our citizens have been privileged to see their superior work."(12) "....It is doubtful that any other organization in America can attract as many recognized stage notables to its ranks than the Stuart Walker company."(13) "....that a repertory company can, and that Stuart Walker's company frequently has, put on productions that excel...has been evidenced time and again."(14)

But, as Tucker observed in Indianapolis, there never seemed to be enough superlatives, and nothing seemed to mellow Walker's suspicion toward those whom he perceived to be against him. In a letter to Sayler, written when Walker's frustration with the eventual decline of the Cincinnati company must have been at its worst, he complained of two local journalists, charging one with provincialism and the other with "Shubertism" [read commercialism]. The tone of the letter demonstrates a desperate callousness and betrays an impulsive need to articulate his anger and give vent to his legendary volatility. He charges that "Golden [does he mean Goldenburg?] has a pigeonhole mind and that's all that he can use....It seems to be the way of the smaller cities of the world to believe....nothing [good] about home people." That was in 1931. In the same letter he wrote: "By the way, the critic on the

Cincinnati Enquirer....was killed the other day in an accident. Perhaps there may now be less Shubert and more theatre in the Enquirer for the future."(15) This seems particularly harsh even for a man who always spoke before thinking when he was in a temper. Walker may well have been bipolar in any era when that problem was not recognized, much less treated.

Long before the October 1929 opening, Cincinnati was primed for Walker's tenth season. The Taft Theater financed a renovation which included the addition of equipment to assist the hard of hearing, a significant and unusual service not even standard in many of today's houses. *Peter Ibbetson* (an old John Barrymore vehicle) was announced as the gala production, and subscription patrons were rewarded with a 20% discount. (Regular top price was $20.00 a season for box seats.) Walker often revived a good box-office title and George Du Maurier's *Ibbetson* had been presented five seasons earlier in both Indianapolis and Cincinnati with George Somnes and MacKay Morris. Both actors returned by popular demand to reprise their original roles. The large cast was supported by what was called the Stuart Walker Orchestra Ensemble, showing that music remained important to the Walker style.

In the hopeful spring before the anniversary season, the social column of the *Enquirer* reported that 65 men and women gathered for a Sunday afternoon tea at "Lauderdale," the home of Mr. and Mrs. George Dent Cribbs, to discuss providing a basis for Walker's company to become permanent in Cincinnati.(16) The coordinators planned to sell stock in the amount of between $150,000 and $200,000 during the summer. Walker doubtless felt that his perseverance had finally paid off when he saw "The Walker Company" legally incorporated in the early fall of 1929. He believed that formal civic and public backing would give the organization a more permanent position in the community, always maintaining that

> in every city there is a great public which
> is eager to know and see the best. There is
> no reason why these people should not be
> organized to make a theatre which will show
> the best drama in the world.(17)

This statement was printed in a promotional flyer for the company that same year. The legally incorporated title was listed as *The Cincinnati Stuart Walker Company*.

The President of the board was Robert L. Black, a prominent attorney and civic leader. Among the more substantial subscribers were Anna Taft, Mrs. George Dent Cribbs, Edgar Friedlander, Charles J. Livingood, and Allen R. Joslin. The business office announced the addition of Arthur Hanna, as assistant manager. Walker traded all his theatrical assets in exchange for stock in the corporation and worked as director on a salary.(18) Of the board supporters, Anna Taft proved to be genuinely interested in the company, as did Charles J. Livingood, who provided a translation for Walker's lavish production of *L'arlesienne* in 1930.

Media promoters were jubilant. "Released of financial responsibility Walker may be permitted to assert himself to the fullest extent,"(19) columnist Goldenburg cheered. "The Enterprise becomes civically important and reflects a new attendance to theater in general." The ancients would have known that it's a mistake to even whisper to the gods that things are going well.

The Walker Company schedule did not skip a beat when the stock market hit bottom on October 24, 1929. Nor did the local stage managers' strike (which was not settled till January of 1930) seem to affect the morale of either the Taft or the company. On October 28, Somerset Maugham's *Our Betters* opened with guest artist Florence Reed in the leading role. Miss Reed returned in November to play in

East of Suez. She played to a large opening night crowd and gave a curtain speech thanking Walker for the opportunity. A highlight of the 1929 season was the American premiere of Casella's *Death Takes a Holiday* which Lee Shubert produced at the Ethel Barrymore in 1930 with a different creative team. (The plot has enjoyed a long popularity most recently surfacing as a Brad Pitt film.)

Apparently Walker felt that things were going well enough to install a two-week run and embark upon a lecture tour for himself. He appeared in Kentucky and Chicago talking to civic drama organizations and felt that the shows back in Cincinnati were doing fine without him.

Walker offered several well-produced scripts of classic value in 1930. Blanche Yurka again was featured in January in *L'arlesienne* and the same year she appeared in Ibsen's *Wild Duck* which was hailed artistically from all sides. In March, Walker presented a special one-week engagement of Bonstelle's version of *Little Women* and in April, mounted Philip Barry's *The Youngest* which had been considered one of New York's better 1924 scripts. (His most stimulating competition was William Gillette's farewell tour of *Secret Service* at the Grand Opera House.) No matter what, by the late spring it was apparent that the season was sagging. Newspapers protested that the company could never fail completely or go into dissolution, but a combination of economic problems was about to descend on the corporation.

J. J. Shubert's prophecy for the resuscitation of stock didn't come to pass and even the Shubert houses were all converting to film. The general consensus was that the public felt that entertainment provided by actors could be just as efficiently presented on film as on the stage. (Now that film has come into its own as an art form it is easier to see that these two genres utilize completely separate conventions and techniques and afford different experiences, but in the early days of film the public put the two into one category.)

Walker seemed oblivious to the economic climate and "for a full year after the crash he counted on making money on anything he chose to present,"[20] observed the *New York Times* in a 1932 article. If the danger signals were out, no one in the Walker organization paid much attention to them.

By 1932 Walker was being courted (and to a great extent enjoying it) by Hollywood. He had sent a letter to his Board President Black urging against any attempt to plan a 1931-32 season. He asked that the Taft be released to any other companies that might need the space and, of course, ended with a parting shot that said "the public may be in a better humor to greet us when they find we are not so available." He continued and complained that the "amount owing to me was diminished by many thousands....Is it really the will of the directors that I should have been....allowed to suffer such unexpected financial blows? I am not yet out of debt...." He concluded the same letter by advising discretion since "the details of our business are not the affair of anyone outside our corporation."[21]

It is easier to discuss reasons for the failure of the Cincinnati company than for that of Indianapolis. The stock market crash, which occurred only a few days after the season opening, had a profound effect on the stability of the fledgling board of directors. The company roster of actors fell from 71 to 29, and although there are no production figures available, it is safe to assume that each show took a substantial budget cut. If Anna Taft had not come to the rescue by underwriting the deficit, the company might have gone under that same season. She was widowed in January of 1930 and often attended the Monday afternoon dress rehearsals, finding the company membership to be a warm and welcoming extended family. The death of Mrs. Taft in February of 1931 left the company without a patron. The board was apparently unable or unwilling to pick up the pieces. Walker still might have overcome these problems if he had not also found himself in conflict with a new generation of Broadway tours. A stagehand's strike in New York, along with the effects of the crash, had motivated New York producers to send out a series of star packages. A sampling of those tours reveals popular draws such as the Lunts in *Elizabeth the Queen*, Ethel Barrymore in *Scarlet Sister Mary* and Nazimova in *A Month in the Country*. These proved to be heavyweight competition and although Walker featured plays such as *The Royal Family* and *Fashion* with names as popular as Victor Jory and Beulah Bondi, it was too late to salvage a financially unstable year and a half.

From September 1922 to the spring of 1931, Walker had given Cincinnati eleven seasons — some of those without ever taking a week off. They had played two hundred and sixty-two weeks, two hundred and twenty-one plays, two thousand three hundred and fifty performances. It wasn't enough — the dream was over.

Chapter Six — Hollywood Denouement

IN THE ENTERTAINMENT WORLD, perhaps more than any other profession, Darwin's law of "adapt or die" reigns supreme. Dancers who have passed their prime must either become choreographers or open a studio; ingenues who have made one trip too many to the refrigerator can grow into character roles or start a talent agency; performers whose personality is no longer *au courant* may translate the power of their charm into media endorsements or go into politics; and ex-stage executives who in 1930 insist that motion pictures should "mind their own business and interfere with the painter, not with the theatre"(1) might, in 1931, find themselves employed by the film industry to correct that perception.

There is no readily available explanation as to how Walker first acquired employment in Hollywood. He was friends with a Los Angeles cinematographer who might have recommended his work to the studios. There was also a great wave of stage performers going into the "talkies" at this time, and some were old "Walkerites" such as Elizabeth Patterson and Basil Rathbone who would have joined in supporting his move to greener pastures. Most of all, Walker was not one to sit passively by in the face of adversity. He saw the opportunities in the West and hustled to become a part of a new and thriving entertainment industry.

Whatever the specifics, Walker seemed to be at the most difficult and most admirable moment of his life. He was venturing into a medium where he had little experience, to a city where he had few connections, into an industry where networking was vital. After having been his own master for 16 years, after enjoying a distinguished reputation in the legitimate stage community, after seeing his incorporated civic theater fail just as it was begun, he was willing to start at the bottom of a new professional hierarchy and work his way up. Yet, like Don Quixote, for whom the pursuit (rather than the attainment) of the ideal identifies the pure in heart, he asked that a clause be written into his Hollywood contract permitting him to resign in the event that the Stuart Walker Company of Cincinnati found the funds to resume playing.

Walker's first assignment from B.P. Shulberg, managing director of production, was to groom Paramount's most promising young contract players for stardom. His enthusiasm was predictable and he immediately had the studio equip a special training sound stage. Among his first eight students were Frances Dee (who had just been promoted out of the extra ranks), Randolph Scott (who was to be the studio's next Gary Cooper), and Cary Grant (who had just finished *Blonde Venus* with Marlene Dietrich). An unpublished Paramount press release says that the room designed by their new star-maker [Walker] was built to challenge the actors with every kind of set device they might normally encounter: "the drawing room had five windows, each different from the other...seven types of doors...a dozen types of chairs and sofas, and scores of small hand props."(2) He felt that this experience shortened rehearsal time once filming began. He also made screen tests on a regular basis using different lenses to make actors aware of long, medium, and close-up shots and of the technique necessary for each. In a similar release he is quoted as saying that "mental, physical, and spiritual health are the three most important things for an actor," adding that a young actor's "interest must be more on the art of acting than on the financial side."(3)

He soon learned how difficult it was to keep the actors long enough to teach them anything. "I was engaged to teach untrained juveniles and ingenues to act," Walker explained, "and if I had been let alone I might have accomplished something." It was a movieland reality that once a face became popular, the studio had to capitalize on that fame and the student was quickly out of the classroom and into the arena of fan mail and maximum exposure. "Even if they have the inclination to attend class, they lack the time" he complained, "and it doesn't so much matter whether a young actor can hold his new won fame or not. His life is estimated roughly at five years....If he falls by the wayside, ah well, there are many others to take his place."(4)

It was not long before Walker was given a chance to prove his skills as a director as well as a coach. Perhaps some of his students' screen tests demonstrated Walker's talent because in the spring of 1931 Jesse L. Lasky, first vice-president in charge of production, announced that Walker, "who was the leading exponent of the repertory theatre in America" and "widely known for his ability to discover and develop young actors...has been signed to direct Paramount Pictures."(5) Walker's appointment was a tribute to his reputation. In comparison to the great number of stage actors brought from the East to work in the talkies, directors fared less well and "out of 244 active directors...only 21 had been brought"(6) from the legitimate stage. The median earnings of a first-year film director at that time was probably under $10,000.

Walker's directorial assignments were usually "B" pictures. Leo Rosten writes that "a studio might produce 20 to 30 'B' films," each made with "speed, economy, and a total disregard for ethics."(7) Walker's "B" films differed from most in two significant ways: he used the same care to mount a film as he did to produce a play and his casts were often made up of excellent actors and well-known film names. This was a period when contract actors, no matter how famous, were committed to a certain number of films of the studio's choosing. If they refused a script because they felt it was inferior they were subject to suspension without pay. It seems possible that the studio depended on

Walker to make bigger names more comfortable with lesser scripts because of his legitimate reputation and because of the attention he accorded the artist. Walker would have been more likely to view the actors as part of the creative process instead of just a shadow on the moviola in the editing room. "It is still better" he said, "to see the stage's old war horses in the pictures — overacting, perhaps, but doing it with a fine, sure touch."(8)

His first picture was *The Woman* (based on the Belasco play), starring Richard Arlen. This was followed by *False Madonna* with William Boyd (later television's *Hopalong Cassidy*) and Kaye Francis, *The Misleading Lady* with Claudette Colbert and Edmund Lowe, *Evenings for Sale* with Herbert Marshall, *Tonight is Ours* with Colbert and Frederic March, *White Woman* with Charles Laughton and Carole Lombard, and *The Eagle and the Hawk* with Cary Grant and Fredric March. In a very short time Walker had directed many of Paramount's most enduring talents! All of the leading players listed above became major draws for their studio. That he was of immediate value to the studio was clear when his *Bulldog Drummond* brought them out of the red.... He surprised everybody on the lot by bringing two pictures in at the same time under budget and well-received.

In 1934 and 1935 he directed a few films for Universal, the foremost being two versions of Dickens' novels: *The Mystery of Edwin Drood*, starring Claude Rains as John Jasper, and *Great Expectations* with Henry Hull, Alan Hale, Jane Wyatt, and Florence Reed. At *Drood's* opening, *Variety* commended Walker for bringing "life and color to this Charles Dickens mellerdrama"(9) and the *Motion Picture Herald* found it "an attention-gripping picture characterized by able execution and excellent performances." *The Hollywood Reporter* was even more effusive toward *Great Expectations*, calling Walker's "direction in perfect taste" and declaring the film a success "in every department of its production."(10) It is an interesting side light that

Universal issued study guides (in collaboration with the National Council of Teachers of English) to schools which took their classes to view *Great Expectations*. The guides were extensive and included discussion topics for use before reading the book, before seeing the film, and for comparison and contrast afterward. Whether or not Walker contributed information to the study guides is unknown, but it certainly seems like the kind of project that would have interested him.

Jane Wyatt, who played the young Estella in "Great Expectations" remembers Walker as

> easy to work with and good at his job. I had just come out of New York and knew very little about acting for the movies. He was wonderfully patient.(11)

In one of the few collected references to Walker's adopted son Arthur, Wyatt recalls in the same letter that "Stuart had a son who took me out a couple of times."(12) So Arthur made the California move with Walker and continued to live either near or with him. (13)

Wyatt is best remembered for her 1950's television role in *Father Knows Best* and also as Mr. Spock's mother in the original *Star Trek* as well as the *Star Trek IV* film.

At Universal, Walker continued to get publicity even by accident. While working on *Sing Me A Love Song* he fell from a film lot ramp directing a night club scene and fractured his ankle. The studio devised a special wheel chair for him and he continued to work on the film.

But Walker could not forget the legitimate theater. Whenever interviewed, he always got around to commenting on the development or the demise of the stage, describing the theater as "a victim of real estate. If the big theatrical companies operated just one theater out of town...and developed one winning play it would pay for everything," he argued, "and you've no idea what it means for an actor to have a home base." He condemned the theater for

> not developing raw material...All that any American actor needs is a chance to learn his business [and] an actor has a quarter of a chance of learning anything in a long-run play than he would have even in cheap stock... It is a very strange thing that if you paint in a certain way, it's technique. But if you act in a certain way, it's only a bag of tricks.(14)

Walker set about becoming a Californian, buying a home on North Whittier Drive in Beverly Hills, and was eager to talk to the press about his "central music room, fireplace, four-poster bed, and quilt made by his ancestress, Matilda Beattaille Taliaferro Marshall of Augusta, Kentucky."(15)

However, a set of letters to an old friend, Joseph Graham, in Bellevue, Kentucky exposed a longing for the river towns of his youth. He contacted Graham in hopes of gathering furniture and authentic pieces to reproduce part of a steamboat cabin in one room of his Beverly Hills home. He was looking at Frank Grayson's river history and Charles Ludwig's book on the American canal system to provide background for his search. "My love for the river has been a lasting one," he wrote, "and some day I hope to have time to take a towboat trip from Pittsburgh to New Orleans or maybe to get a launch and take the trip with a few friends."(16)

In 1936 he returned to Paramount to produce. Producers had "a very narrow authority," says Rosten, "but as a group, they possessed more power than any other group in the movie colony."(17) Walker felt comfortable with the position of Associate Producer which enabled him to have some influence over the film and to work with the director on the story. His most distinctive work as Associate Producer was on a film which was already close to his heart, *Seventeen*. It starred Jackie Cooper as Willy Baxter and Betty Field as Lola Pratt and received a maximum of publicity as well as a good box office return. The *L.A. Times* said that this film "safely holds its place with the [Andy] Hardy series."(18) That is solid praise. Mickey Rooney's *Andy Hardy* films were very popular. For a man of sentiment, the product and its reception must have meant a great deal.

Analyses of Walker films remain divided. *The Eagle and the Hawk* seems to have garnered the most serious praise as "an outstandingly frank war film...with several disturbing scenes graphically depicted in uncompromising shots."(19) The film was listed in the top ten movies of at least one critic's yearly inventory.

Yet the film colony and Stuart Walker never really made a comfortable match. His films were never blockbusters; they never "clicked with the great rank and file of cinematics," concluded critic Robert Tucker, "but as a developer of talent for the stage he stood in the very front ranks."(20) And perhaps Walker subconsciously harbored the same feeling that many of his generation did toward the films:

> ...the actors in the cinema are dead. The audience is looking at and listening to not what they are doing, but what they have done some time ago; and no reaction from the audience can modify their performance by a hair's breath.(21)

Nor did he ever quite forget the dream: "there is now no place in the English-speaking world where young actors and young playwrights can be developed in that [stock] way. And the need is so bad you can almost taste it."(22) But even Walker admitted that he was no longer the man to make it happen. A melancholy admission that:

> The theatre needs the fire of youth. When I was a young man I went ahead and trusted to God to find a way of paying the bills. I will say this too, things turned out all right. But now I have reached an age -- shall we call it fairly mature? -- that needs financial security.(23)

He said he missed the Cincinnati Red Legs, he said his things were still in storage in Cincinnati, he said he thought he might like to direct in New York again.

In December of 1940 Walker suffered a cerebral hemorrhage. After an apparent improvement in his condition he was sent home from the hospital. He developed pneumonia and subsequently died of a heart attack at his home on March 13, 1941, nine days after his birthday. The *Cincinnati Times-Star* called his company "the foremost resident company in America."(24) The *New York Times* referred to him as a "prominent film producer, playwright, and founder of the Portmanteau Theatre."(25) In a *Times-Star* interview, Robert Black, who served as board president of the ill-fated Cincinnati company, proclaimed him successful in "making this city a notable center for the art of the speaking stage — a center outside of New York."(26) He would have enjoyed the coverage. But no one could speak as eloquently as the one hundred and fifty or more successful actors whose careers he launched, nurtured, and molded. The Actors' Guild produced a memorial on May 28, 1941 by presenting *The Medicine Show*, *The Birthday of the Infanta*, *The Very Naked Boy*, and *Nevertheless*, a tribute Walker would have appreciated.

Epilogue — Memory

STUART WALKER EXERCISED A GENUINE INFLUENCE in several areas of the theater. His scripts and adaptations are still produced; his contribution in keeping the stock tradition alive insured that a generation of performers and audience members shared in the realization of an accessible, affordable, quality theater experience; his Portmanteau became a part of "little theatre" history in America; and during a lifetime in the arts he shared his professional philosophies and practices with hundreds of film and stage performers who, in turn, influenced other artists. Although he did not realize his primary goal of a permanent Midwestern repertory circuit, he did most certainly achieve a goal shared by every stage professional: he made an impact on and worked in his chosen field until the day he died. In this profession, that is the definition of success. He did so not only because he was a multitalented individual, but also because he was willing to persevere, to adapt, and to take risks, all qualities necessary for success in any profession.

A credible concluding chapter must cite more than just the statistical achievements of Walker's career. He was a respected member of a small and demanding profession, and it was this quality of professionalism together with his mercurial personality which makes him attractive to the reader. His volatile nature revealed a passion for his craft that he balanced with a tireless work ethic. His loyalty to coworkers was as strong as his impatience with those who were without commitment. His temperament, as much as his exploits, made it possible for him to earn a place in the record books.

He appears to have been an extremely private person. Although he fought constantly for company publicity there are few moments of personal reflection in interviews; most comments, even in letters, relate to business. His public persona was the best role he ever created. Neither is there any mention of hobbies in the press or his correspondence. Until Arthur, the company was his only family and even after the adoption, he still spent his most significant hours with them.

Since there is no past without memory, it is in the memory of others that any historical figure ultimately meets his fate. The material documented in the preceding chapters is selected memory. Even critical reviews represent a recollected response "recorded in the briefest of prose [subject to] many distortions of the truth."(1) And so, like Memory walking down the aisles of Walker's old Portmanteau, I choose to end this volume with those memories belonging to his audience — those theatrical partners whom Walker described as indispensable to the future of the art form. These are the individuals who acquire the wisdom through collaborating in the arts to make their community tolerant, humane, stimulating, sensitive, aware and, in short, civilized. "The standing of a city depends," Walker was fond of saying, "upon the cultural advantages it offers in music, art, educational facilities and the theater as well as upon its industrial supremacy."(2)

Though more than two generations have passed since Walker's death, it was still possible to find individuals who remember the influence that Walker Company productions had on their lives. Ruth Nimitz, in her 80's during a 1996 interview, remembered her theater visits as "such a happy, innocent time in our lives. I went to a convent school and my parents never worried about the plays I went to see as a teen. When I married," she added, "I didn't stop going; my husband and I went every Thursday night."(3) Dr. David Zemsky was the youngest of three brothers who ushered at the Cox in 1924. "We came from a poor district, a ghetto almost," he recalled, "and the theater was a great world opening up to us. Mr. Walker was very professional — and that's a word whose meaning I've learned."(4)

Professional is an excellent word to add to those which best describe Walker: professional, perfectionist, workaholic, survivor, and most of all — dreamer.

CHAPTER NOTES

CHAPTER ONE

1) The William Chapman family had long been a theatrical tradition in England. They toured through the United Kingdom and then came to America to continue that tradition. They chose to keep it alive by establishing Chapman's Floating Theatre in 1831. That first showboat was a flatboat one hundred feet long by sixteen feet wide and was built in Pittsburgh especially for Chapman.

2) The Bryants: Billy, Florence, Violet and Sam, started out in medicine shows and vaudeville. Their first showboat experience was in Augusta, Kentucky and they continued on to perform in several cities on the Ohio River and to add one more generation of performers to their floating family.

3) Most obituaries list Walker as 53 at the time of his death in 1941 which places him at the younger end of the controversial span. Earlier related documentation (including the American Academy of Dramatic Arts' records) argues against a birth date after 1880, and it seems reasonable that, as a public figure, he simply obscured his actual date of birth as he grew older.

4) *Cincinnatian.* University of Cincinnati Yearbook, 1899 to 1903. College-Conservatory of Music Library. University of Cincinnati.

5) Fields, William A. "Stuart Walker, Noted Figure in American Theater, Will Head His Company in Final Play of Season." *Indianapolis Star* August 28, 1927: Sec. 7:2.

6) Shakespeare, William. *Complete Works*. David Bevington, Ed. New York: Longman, 1997. Act I, scene i.

7) American Academy of Dramatic Arts Audition Record Book, April 3, 1908. Pages 178-179, signed by Franklin Haven Sargent.

8) McSweeney, Meg. Letter to the author. January 24, 1996.

9) Davis, Ronald J. *Augustus Thomas*. Boston: G.K. Hall & Company, 1984.

10) "Mr. Walker Looks Back." *New York Times* February 7, 1932.

11) Clark, Constance and Mari Kathleen Fielder. "Jessie Bonstelle." *Notable Women in the American Theatre*. Alice M. Robinson, Vera Mowry Roberts, and Milly S. Barranger, eds. New York: Greenwood, 1989. 76-82.

12) Storey, Margaret and Hugh Gillis. *Players' Nursery*. Stanford: Dramatist's Alliance, 1940.

13) Holmes, Ralph. "Back Stage Story." *Detroit Journal* July 30, 1921.

CHAPTER TWO

1) Brooks, Katherine. Untitled Clipping. *Boston Evening Record* February, 1916. SW Coll. Billy Rose.

2) "Drama League of America Cincinnati Center takes pride in presenting Stuart Walker's Portmanteau Theatre in a repertory of plays to its members and other students and devotees of the art of theatre in

Cincinnati. It comes to Cincinnati after a pronounced success in other cities, where its artistic results have received much favorable comment." Inside the program. No date noted.

3) Untitled clipping. *Munsey's Magazine* October, 1915. Indiana State Library Reference Division.

4) Mackay, Constance D'Arcy. *The Little Theatre in the United States.* New York: Holt, 1917.

5) Walker also planned, while at Christadora, to conduct what we now call "outreach" by directing the settlement children in private performances, but there is no indication that this ever happened. He did, however, give a free performance of *The Seven Gifts* at Madison Square Garden on Christmas night 1915, and continued to give free performances to children in many cities during his years of touring under the Portmanteau banner.

6) "Stuart Walker Discusses Stock Company." *Billboard Magazine.* December 8, 1928: 104.

7) Bierstadt, Edward Hale. *Portmanteau Plays.* By Stuart Walker. Cincinnati: Stewart Kidd, 1921. iii-xl.

8) Tucker, Robert G. "Mr. Walker's Tenth Season Opening at Keith's Monday." Indianapolis Star May 6, 1928, Sec. 7.

9) "The Stage." *Baltimore Evening Sun* 1924. SW Coll. Billy Rose.

10) Walker, Stuart. "The Spirit of Youth Behind the Footlights." *Theatre Magazine* (February 1918) 27: 75-76.

11) "Theater Too Elaborate: Mr. Walker Predicts Return to Simplicity." *Boston Advisor* February 11, 1916.

12) Abbey, Lorenzo. Untitled Clipping Suburban Society Magazine March, 1916. SW Coll. Billy Rose.

13) "Why Go to the Theater?" *Pittsburgh Post* December 24, 1916. SW Coll. Billy Rose.

14) Walker, Stuart. *Portmanteau Plays*. Ed. with intro. by Edward Hale Bierstadt. Cincinnati: Stewart Kidd. 1919.

15) Untitled Clipping. *New York Evening Weekly* April 30, 1917. SW Coll. Billy Rose.

16) Column, Padraic. Introduction. *A Dreamer's Tales and Other Stories*. By Lord Dunsany. New York: Boni & Liveright, 1917.

17) Quoted in Sayler, Oliver M. "Lord Dunsany." *Boston Evening Transcript*: October 212, 1916. SW Coll. Billy Rose.

18) Bierstadt, Edward Hale. *Dunsany the Dramatist*. Boston: Little Brown, 1917.

19) Sayler, Oliver M. "Lord Dunsany." *Boston Evening Transcript* October 21, 1916. SW Coll. Billy Rose.

20) Sayler, Oliver M. "Lord Dunsany." *Boston Evening Transcript* October 21, 1916. SW Coll. Billy Rose.

21) Brooks, Katherine. Untitled Clipping. *Boston Evening Record* February, 1916. SW Coll. Billy Rose.

22) Untitled clipping. *Theater Arts Magazine* circa 1917. SW Coll. Billy Rose.

23) Box Office Report. Cincinnati Grand Theatre, circa 1917. SW Coll. Billy Rose.

24) Kidd Dramatic Publications Flyer. SW Coll. Billy Rose.

25) "Stuart Walker Aims to Restore Youth to Theater." *Christian Science Monitor* February 14, 1916.

26) "Birthday of the Infanta." *Detroit Journal* 1917. SW Coll. Billy Rose.

27) "The Chronicler." *Dayton News* January 14, 1917. SW Coll. Billy Rose.

28) "Children of Institutions are Guests of Drama League." *Pittsburgh Dispatch* November 11, 1916.

29) "In the Wake of the Portmanteau Theatre." *Cleveland Leader* January 14, 1917.

30) Portmanteau Publicity flyer. February, circa 1917. SW Coll. Billy Rose.

31) Untitled Clipping, *Columbus Journal* December 17, 1916. SW Coll. Billy Rose.

32) Warsden, Rancholt. "Little Theatre and Big Ideas." *Theatre Magazine* 25 (February 1917): 92.

33) "Time." *New York Times* December 1923. SW Coll. Billy Rose.

34) The song "New York, New York" is from the film of the same title. John Kander, composer and Fred Ebb, lyricist collaborated first on the musical *Flora, the Red Menace* which was not a financial success although it did present Liza Minelli in an auspicious debut. Their first hit was *Cabaret* and they went on to write *Chicago*, *Woman of the Year* and *Steel Pier* among others.

35) Bierstadt, Edward Hale. "Repertory Theater in America." *Brentano's Book Chat* October, 1921. SW Coll. Billy Rose.

CHAPTER THREE

1) "Local Stock Companies are Gaining Importance Says Walker." *Detroit Times* December 10, 1924. SW Coll. Billy Rose.

2) Walker, Stuart. Letter to Oliver M. Sayler. November 30, 1930. SW Coll. Billy Rose.

3) Walker, Stuart. Letter to Oliver M. Sayler. November 13, 1930. SW Coll. Billy Rose.

4) Thompson, Glenn. "Stuart Walker Homesick; Follows Reds Progress." *Cincinnati Enquirer* March 12, 1939: 3-4.

5) Walker, Stuart. Letter to Robert Garland. August 20, 1931. SW Coll. Billy Rose.

6) Anderson, Jean Jory. Telephone interview. November 27, 1995.

7) Sayler, Oliver M. "Stuart Walker and His Theater." *New York Herald Tribune* Item #126, Holliday Coll. CHS.

8) Jackson, Richard Scott. "Stuart Walker and Company: Broadway in the Middlewest." Thesis. Purdue University, 1958.

9) "Seventeen Will Make Its First Bow Tonight to Indianapolis Public." *Indianapolis Star* June 18, 1917.

10) "Show Shop." *Indianapolis Star* August 14, 1917.

11) Walker, Stuart. Letter to Oliver M. Sayler. November 23, 1930. SW Coll. Billy Rose.

12) Towse, Ranken. "Job." *New York Evening Post* May 17, 1919.

13) Walker, Stuart. Letter to the editor. *Indianapolis Star*. October 12, 1922. SW Coll. Billy Rose.

14) Hermcheil, William. Untitled Clipping, *Indianapolis News* July 3, 1920: 15-16.

15) Hermcheil, William. Untitled Clipping, *Indianapolis News* July 3, 1920: 15-16.

16) Walker, Stuart. Letter to Beulah Bondi. December 15, 1924. Beulah Bondi file. Margaret Herrick.

17) Gaul, George. Letter to Percy Hammond: "Oddiments and Remainders." 1924. SW Coll. Billy Rose.

18) "English's Has a Good One." *Indianapolis News* August 13, 1918: 7.

19) Baker, Tarkington. "From the Viewpoint of the Arctic." *Indianapolis Star* August 1, 1918.

20) "Dunsany in Gripsack." *New York Times* February 9, 1919.

21) "Kismet." *Indianapolis Star* July 1, 1919.

22) Jackson, Richard Scott. "Stuart Walker and Company: Broadway in the Middle West." Thesis. Purdue University, 1958.

23) Yurka, Blanche. *Bohemian Girl.* Athens: Ohio University Press, 1970.

24) Jory, Jon. Telephone interview. November 18, 1995.

25) Anderson, Jean Jory. Telephone interview. November 27, 1995.

26) "School for Scandal." *Indianapolis News* August 1, 1922.

27) "Wedding Bells." *Indianapolis Star* August 7, 1921.

28) "Honors are Even." *Indianapolis Star* May 1, 1922.

29) Jackson, Richard Scott. "Stuart Walker and Company: Broadway in the Middle West." Thesis. Purdue University, 1958.

30) "Ibbetson." *Indianapolis Star* July 24, 1923.

31) Untitled Clipping, *Indianapolis Star* September, 1923. Indiana State Library Reference Division, item #100-730.

32) Caldwell, Howard. "Summer Stock with Stuart Walker." *Indianapolis Magazine*. October, 1976: 56-57.

33) Walker, Stuart. Letter to Robert Tucker of *Indianapolis Star*. November 23, 1923. SW Coll. Billy Rose.

34) Hickman, Walter D. "Stuart Walker Blames the Press and Public." *Indianapolis Times* August 1, 1928.

35) Tucker, Robert G. "Closing--Stuart Walker Season." *Indianapolis Star*. August 5, 1928.

36) Tucker, Robert G. "Closing--Stuart Walker Season." *Indianapolis Star*. August 5, 1928.

37) Caldwell, Howard. "Summer Stock with Stuart Walker." *Indianapolis Magazine*. October, 1976. 56-57.

CHAPTER FOUR

1) Goldenburg, William Smith. "Theater" *Cincinnati Enquirer* September 16, 1926.

2) Clark, Constance and Mari Kathleen Fielder. "Jessie Bonstelle." *Notable Women in the American Theatre.* Alice M. Robinson, Vera Mowry Roberts, and Milly S. Barranger, eds. New York: Greenwood, 1989. 76-82.

3) Jory, Jon. Telephone interview. December 11, 1995.

4) Jory, Jon. Telephone interview. November 27, 1995.

5) Fergusson, Francis. "America Between the Wars." *The Human Image in Dramatic Literature.* New York: Doubleday, 1957. 5-22.

6) Cheney, Sheldon. *The Art Theatre.* New York: Knopf, 1969.

7) Cheney, Sheldon. *The Art Theatre.* New York: Knopf, 1969.

8) Barnes, Howard. Untitled Clipping *New York Journal Tribune.* March 9, no year. SW Coll. Billy Rose.

9) A comparative listing of the 1924 season titles at three stock/repertory companies:

> DETROIT CIVIC: *It Happened, Up the Ladder, So This is London, The Breaking Point, What A Wife, Secrets, You and I, That Awful Mrs. Eaton, Leah Kleschna, The Claw and the Wing, Paolo and Francesca,* and *Helena's Boys.* (Storey/Gillis I, xii)

HEDGEROW: *Androcles and the Lion, The Artist, Beyond the Horizon, Candida, Cast Up by the Sea, The Dragon, Dreamers, The Emperor Jones, The Heart of Youth, The Hero, The Inheritors, King Hunger, March Hares, The Master Builder, Misalliance, Mr. Pim Passes By, The Pillars of Society, Paolo and Francesca, Richard II, Rollo's Wild Oat,* and *His Honor the Mayor.*

WALKER'S CINCINNATI COX: *The Proud Princess, Main Street, Polly Preferred, Kempy, If I Were King, Why Men Leave Home, The Importance of Being Earnest, Trelawney of the Wells, Icebound, My Lady's Dress, The Goldfish, Three Wise Fools, Clarence, Liliom, You and I, The Hero, Three Roses, The Boomerang, Old Heidelberg, Pot Luck, Lady Windermere's Fan, The First Year, Mary the Third, The Thunderbolt, The Night Cup, You Never Can Tell, Spanish Love, The Proud Princess (re-mount), Just Suppose, Outward Bound, Nothing But the Truth, Too Many Cooks,* and *A Little Journey.*

CHAPTER FIVE

1) Thuman, J. H. "Theater." *Cincinnati Enquirer.* April 21, 1918. Box 10 Folder 9, Holliday Coll. CHS.

2) "Walker Players as a Local Enterprise." *Cincinnati Commercial Tribune* June 2, 1922.

3) "Walker Players as a Local Enterprise." *Cincinnati Commercial Tribune* June 2, 1922.

4) "Stock Coming Back Opines J. J. Shubert." *Variety* September 28, 1923. SW Coll. Billy Rose.

5) Untitled Clipping. *New York Morning Telegraph* December 1, 1923. SW Coll. Billy Rose.

6) "Main Street." *Theatre Magazine* December 1921: 387

7) Goldenburg, William Smith. "Walker Season Closes." *Cincinnati Enquirer* September 5, 1926. Holliday Coll. CHS.

8) "Stuart Walker May Not Return." *Cincinnati Commercial Tribune* September 27, 1926.

9) "Stage vs. Screen." *Cincinnati Times-Star.* June 25, 1927. SW Coll. Billy Rose.

10) Untitled Clipping, *Cincinnati Enquirer* December 2, 1928. SW Coll. Billy Rose.

11) Untitled Clipping, *Cincinnati Enquirer* December 2, 1928. SW Coll. Billy Rose.

12) "Walker Players at Strand." *Huntington Dispatch/Advisor* October 27, 1926. SW Coll. Billy Rose.

13) Elliston, George. "Cincinnatian in Hollywood." *Cincinnati Times-Star* May 23, 1938: 11.

14) "Stuart Walker Productions Fully Up to Thespian Standards of Broadway." *Dayton Journal* August 17, 1924. SW Coll. Billy Rose.

15) Walker, Stuart. Letter to Oliver M. Sayler. September 15, 1931. SW Coll. Billy Rose.

16) "In Society." *Cincinnati Enquirer* April 30, 1929: 11 Holliday Coll. CHS.

17) Walker Cincinnati Company promotional flyer. Theatre folder Misc. 3. Holliday Coll. CHS.

18) Holliday, Joseph E. "Stuart Walker's Cincinnati Theater." *Cincinnati Historical Society* Bulletin 35, No. 3 Fall, 1977. 150-172.

19) "More on Strike." *Cincinnati Enquirer* October 13, 1929. Box 9 Holliday Coll. CHS.

20) "The Mystery of Edwin Drood." *Motion Picture Herald*. March 30, 1935. Stuart Walker file, Margaret Herrick.

21) Walker, Stuart. Letter to Robert Black. September 28, 1931. #199 Holliday Coll. CHS.

CHAPTER SIX

1) "Stuart Walker, 53, Producer, is Dead." *New York Times* March 14, 1941.

2) Paramount Studios unpublished press release #19986. Stuart Walker file. Margaret Herrick.

3) Paramount Studios unpublished press released #175335. Stuart Walker File. Margaret Herrick.

4) Soanes, Wood. "Ex-Lumberjack Directs Screen Productions and Holds Class in Acting." Hollywood circa 1931. Stuart Walker file, Margaret Herrick.

5) Paramount Studios Western Union Press Release. Signed by Earl Wingart. March 5, 1931. Stuart Walker file. Margaret Herrick.

6) Rosten, Leo C. *Hollywood: The Movie Colony*. New York: Harcourt, 1941.

7) Rosten, Leo C. *Hollywood: The Movie Colony*. New York: Harcourt, 1941.

8) "Mr. Walker Looks Back." *New York Times*. February 7, 1932.

9) "Pictures: Mystery of Edwin Drood." Variety March 27, 1935. Stuart Walker file, Margaret Herrick.

10) "Great Expectations Hit; Writing, Acting, Flawless." *Hollywood Reporter* October 10, 1934.

11) Wyatt, Jane. Letter to the author. March 9, 1996.

12) Wyatt, Jane. Letter to the author. March 9, 1996.

13) An interesting sidelight to an afternoon Wyatt spent with Arthur Helm Walker took place while they were on their way to "the posh Bell Aire Club to swim and to have lunch. Suddenly he [Arthur Walker] threw on the brakes and said, 'Damn, I've just remembered they won't permit actors to come to the club'". Letter to the author.

14) "Mr. Walker Looks Back." *New York Times*. February 7, 1932.

15) Elliston, George. "Cincinnatian in Hollywood." *Cincinnati Times-Star* May 23, 1938: 11.

16) "Walker Planned to Reproduce Steamboat Cabin in His Home." *Cincinnati Times-Star* March 18, 1941.

17) Rosten, Leo C. *Hollywood: The Movie Colony*. New York: Harcourt, 1941.

18) Untitled Clipping. *L.A. Times* February 15, 1940.

19) Quinlan, David. *The Illustrated Guide to Film Directors*. London: Batsford, 1983. 309-310.

20) "Stuart Walker, Ex-Cincinnatian, Playwright and Movie Producer Dies in Beverly Hills." *Cincinnati Times-Star* March 14, 1941.

21) Carr, Philip. Untitled Clipping. *New York Times* July 20, 1930. SW Coll. Billy Rose.

22) "Progress." *Cincinnati Enquirer* March 12, 1939: 3-4.

23) "Progress." *Cincinnati Enquirer* March 12, 1939: 3-4.

24) "Stuart Walker, Ex-Cincinnatian, Playwright and Movie Producer Dies in Beverly Hills." *Cincinnati Times-Star* March 14, 1941.

25) "Stuart Walker, 53, Producer, is Dead." *New York Times* March 14, 1941.

26) "Stuart Walker Rites Will be Held Tuesday." *Cincinnati Times-Star* March 17, 1941.

CHAPTER SEVEN

1) Bentley, Eric. *What is Theater?* New York: Atheneum, 1979.

2) Jennings, Paul. "Stuart Walker--A Cincinnati Institution." *The Cincinnatian Magazine* no month, 1927: 8-9. Holliday Collection. CHS.

3) Nimitz, Ruth. Telephone interview. December 28, 1995.

4) Zemsky, Dr. David. Telephone interview. December 28, 1995.

Appendix I
Indianapolis Stock Company Seasons

Shubert-Murat

Title	Author
1917	
It Pays To Advertise	Roi Cooper Megrue
The Dummy	Harvey O'Higgins
	Harriet Ford
The Concert	David Belasco
The Very Naked Boy	Stuart Walker
Kick In	Willard Mack
Nevertheless	Stuart Walker
Seventeen*	Booth Tarkington
Seven Keys to Baldpate	George M. Cohan
The Country Boy	Edgar Selwyn
The Birthday of the Infanta	adapted by Stuart Walker
You Never Can Tell	G.B. Shaw
Officer 666	Augustin MacHugh
Broadway Jones	George M. Cohan
The Woman	David Belasco
Six Who Pass While the Lentils Boil	Stuart Walker
The Show Shop	James Forbes

1918

The Misleading Lady	Paul Dickey/ Charles Goddard
The Hero*	Alice Brown
Stop Thief	Carlyle Moore
Romance	Edward Sheldon
Alias Jimmy Valentine	Paul Armstrong
Passers-By	C. Haddon Chambers
The Dummy	O'Higgins /Ford
Seven Up*	Alta May Coleman
The Three of Us	Rachel Crothers
The Fortune Hunter	Winchell Smith
Alice-Sit-By-The-Fire	J.M. Barrie
The Workhouse Ward	Lady Gregory
The Wolf	Eugene Walter
The Truth	Clyde Fitch
Jonathan Makes a Wish*	Stuart Walker

1919

The Cinderella Man	Edward Childs Carpenter
Good Gracious Annabelle	Clare Kummer
Leah Keschna	C.M.S. McClellen
The Book of Job	King James version
Over Night	Philip Bartholomae
The Passing of the Third Floor Back	Jerome K. Jerome
Romance	Edward Sheldon
Milestones	Arnold Bennett/ Edward Knoblock
Kismet	Edward Knoblock
Don	Rudolph Besier
The Murders	Lord Dunsany

The Gibson Upright*	Booth Tarkington/ Leon Wilson
Too Many Cooks	Frank Craven
Kick In	Willard Mack
Nothing But the Truth	James Montgomery
Fair and Warmer	Avery Hopwood
The Fortune Hunter	Winchell Smith
Piccadilly Jim	Guy Bolton/ P.G. Wodehouse

1920

Two Kisses	Henry James Smith
Miracle Man	George M. Cohan
Polly With a Past	George Middleton
The Storm Bird*	Dion Clayton Calthrop/ Roland Pertwee
The Show Shop	James Forbes
The Gypsy Trail	Robert Housum
Temperamental Henry*	Samuel Merwin
The Lodger	Horace Amesley Vachell
Baby Mine	Margaret Mayo
The Little Journey	Rachel Crothers
A Very Good Young Man	Martin Brown
Too Many Husbands	Somerset Maugham
Peg O' My Heart	J. Hartley Manners
39 East	Rachel Crothers

1921

The Wolf	Eugene Walter
Mamma's Affair	Rachel Barton Butler

Daddies	John Hobble
Smilin' Through	Allan Langdon Martin
The World and His Wife	Jose Echegaray
Tea for Three	Roi Cooper Megrue
Book of Job	King James version
Come Seven	Octavius Roy Cohen
Nevertheless	Stuart Walker
Six Who Pass While the Lentils Boil	Stuart Walker
Sir David Wears a Crown	Stuart Walker
My Lady Friends	Frank Mandel/ Emil Nytray
*Artists' Life**	Peggy Wood/ Samuel Merwin
A Pair of Silk Stockings	Cyril Harcourt
*Main Street**	adapted by O'Higgins/Ford
Monna Vanna	Maurice Maeterlinck
Two Kisses	Harry James Smith
Trilby	George Du Maurier
The Lottery Man	Rida Johnson Young
*Honor Bright**	Meredith/ Kenyon Nichelson
The Beautiful Adventure	de Flers/de Caillavet

1922

Honors Are Even	Roi Cooper Megrue
Three Live Ghosts	Max Marcin/ Frederick Isham
The Acquittal	Rita Weiman
The Detour	Owen Davis
Captain Kidd, Jr.	Rita Johnson Young
The Boomerang	Winchell Smith/Victor Mapes
Our Little Wife	Avery Hopwood

Matinee only:

Trimplet	Stuart Walker
Six Who Pass	Stuart Walker
Sir David	Stuart Walker
My Lady's Dress	Edward Knoblock
Erstwhile	Susan Marion de Forest
Cornered	Dodson Mitchell
Seven Chances	Roi Cooper Megrue
Here Comes the Bride	Max Marcin/ Roy Atwell
The School for Scandal	Richard Brinsley Sheridan
The Silver Fox	Cosmo Hamilton
The Faith Healer	Alice Duer Miller/ Robert Milton
Girls	Clyde Fitch
Five Flights Up	Stuart Walker
The Gods of the Mountain	Lord Dunsany

1923

Rollo's Wild Oat	Clare Kummer
Mr. Pim Passes By	A.A. Milne
It's A Boy	William A. McGuire
Banco (adaptation)	Clare Kummer
Girl of the Golden West	David Belasco
An Ideal Husband	Oscar Wilde
Smilin' Through	Allan Langdon Martin
Captain Applejack	Walter Hackett
The Ruined Lady	Frances Nordstrom
Nice People	Rachel Crothers
A Very Good Young Man	Martin Brown
Spite Corner	Frank Craven
Peter Ibbetson	George Du Maurier
Enter Madam	Gilda Varesi/ Dolly Byrne

The First Year — Frank Craven
The Bad Man — Porter Emerson Browne
Jonathan Makes a Wish — Stuart Walker
The Dover Road — A.A. Milne

B.F. Keith's

1926

White Collars	Edith Ellis
Candida	G.B. Shaw
Seventh Heaven	Austin Strong
They Knew What They Wanted	Sidney Howard
The Goose Hangs High	Lewis Beach
Applesauce	Barry Conners
Polly Preferred	Guy Bolton
Outward Bound	Sutton Vane
Puppy Love	Adelaide Matthews/ Martha Stanley
The Old Soak	Don Marquis
Magnolia	Booth Tarkington
The Outsider	Dorothy Brandon
The Swan	Ferenc Molnar
The Mountain Man	Clare Kummer

1927

The Road to Yesterday	Beulah Marie Dix/ Evelyn Greenleaf Sutherland
Lazy Bones	Owen Davis
The Patsy	Barry Conners
Pomeroy's Past	Clare Kummer
The Last of Mrs. Cheyney	Frederick Lonsdale
The Enemy	Channing Pollack
The Poor Nut	Elliott Nugent
The Butter & Egg Man	George S. Kaufman
Icebound	Owen Davis
On Approval	Frederick Lonsdale
Kismet	Edward Knoblock

Alias the Deacon	John Hymer/ Leroy Clemons
The Gorilla	Ralph Spence
Rain	John Colton/ Clemence Randolph
The Show-Off	George Kelly
The Wolf	Eugene Walter
Charm	John Kirkpatrick
In Love With Love	Vincent Lawrence
Beggar on Horseback	Marc Connelly/ George Kaufman

1928

Why Marry	Jesse Lynch Williams
The Jest	Sam Benelli
Saturday's Children	Maxwell Anderson
Crime	Sam Shipman/ John Hymer
The Wooden Kimono	John Floyd
Interference	Roland Pertwee/ Harold Dearden
The Dover Road	A.A. Milne
The Firebrand	Edwin Justus Mayer
The Copperhead	Augustus Thomas
The Cardboard Lover	Jacques Duval
The Baby Cyclone	George M. Cohan
Nightstick	John Wray/ Elaine Carrington
Two Girls Wanted	Gladys Unger
Kempy	Elliott Nugent

(Jackson xviii-xxx)

*premiere

Appendix II
Cincinnati Stock Seasons

Cox Theater
April 24, 1922 — September 23, 1922

Title	Author
Honors Are Even	Roi Cooper Megrue
Three Live Ghosts	Max Marcin/ Frederick Isham
Civilian Clothes	Thomas Buchanan
A Little Journey	Rachel Crothers
Too Many Husbands	Somerset Maugham
The Show Shop	James Forbes
Come Seven	Octavius Roy Cohen
Mama's Affair	Rachel Barton Butler
Cornered	Dodson Mitchell
The Boomerang	Winchell Smith/ Victor Mapes
Kick In	Willard Mack
Good Gracious	Annabelle Clare Kummer
Passers-by	Haddon Chambers
Seven Chances	Roi Cooper Megrue
Wedding Bells	Salisbury Fields
The Mountain Man	Clare Kummer
Don	Rudolph Besier
Rollo's Wild Oat	Clare Kummer
The Charm School	Alice Duer Miller/ Robert Milton

Polly With a Past	George Middleton/ Guy Bolton
The Storm Bird	Don Clayton Calthrop/ Melville Burke
Five Flights Up	Stuart Walker
The Tents of the Arabs	Lord Dunsany

March 24, 1923 — September 30, 1923

Adam and Eve	Guy Bolton/George Middleton
A Prince There Was	George M. Cohan
It's A Boy	William McGuire
His House in Order	Arthur Wing Pinero
The Ruined Lady	Frances Nordstrom
On the Hiring Line	O'Higgins/Ford
The Dummy	O'Higgins/Ford
The Girl of the Golden West	David Belasco
An Ideal Husband	Oscar Wilde
Monna Vanna	Maurice Maeterlinck
Banco	adapt. Clare Kummer
Mr. Pim Passes By	A.A. Milne
Captain Applejack	Walter Hackett
Smilin' Through	Allan Langdon Martin
The World and His Wife	Charles Frederick Nirdlinger (adaptation)
Too Many Cooks	Frank Craven
A Little Journey	Rachel Crothers
The Cat and the Canary	John Willard
Magnolia	Booth Tarkington
The Nervous Wreck	Owen Davis
Madame X	Alexander Bisson
Six Cylinder Love	William Anthony McGuire
John the Worm	J.C. and Elliott Nugent
R.U.R.	Karel Kapek

Thank — U	Winchell Smith/ Tom Cushing
Declassee	Zoe Akins
Dead Magic	Kark Kunst/ Stephen Sanford
The Man Who Came Back	Jules Eckert Goodman
It is the Law	Elmer Rice
Chicken Feed	Guy Bolton
Five Flights Up	Stuart Walker
The Lily	David Belasco
Children of the Moon	Martin Flaven
Smilin' Through	Allan Langdon Martin
School for Scandal	Richard Brinsley Sheridan
The Best People	Avery Hopwood/ Thomas Gray
Meet the Wife	Lynn Sterling
In Love With Love	Vincent Lawrence
Spring Cleaning	Frederick Lonsdale
The Goose Hangs High	Lewis Beach
The Whole Town's Talking	John Emerson/ Anita Loos
Badges	Max Marcin/ Edward Hammond
So This is London	Arthur Goodrich
Minick	George Kaufman/ Edna Ferber
The Darling of the Gods	David Belasco/ John Luther Long
Expressing Willie	Rachel Crothers
The Rear Car	E.E. Rose
New Broom	Frank Craven
East is West	Samuel Shipman / John Humer
The Tailor-Made Man	Harry James Smith

April 26 - October 23, 1926

White Collars	Edith Ellis
Candida	G.B. Shaw
The Outsider	Dorothy Brandon
*A Woman Disputed Among Men**	Dennis Clift
Icebound	Owen Davis
Applesauce	Barry Conners
The Masquerader	John Hunter Booth
Cobra	Martin Brown
A Pair of Silk Stockings	Cyril Harcourt
The Swan	Ferenc Molnar
Too Many Husbands	Somerset Maugham
Applesauce	Barry Conners
Come Seven	Octavius Roy Cohen
The Old Soak	Don Marquis
Maids Errant	Robert Housum
Justice	John Galsworthy
Dancing Mothers	Edgar Selwyn/ Edmund Goulding
Love Is Like That	S. N. Behrman/ Kenyon Nicholson
*Beatrice and the Blackguard**	Ernest Goodwin
The Swan	Ferenc Molnar
The Outsider	Dorothy Brandon
*Daughters of Music**	Don Totheroh
Begger on Horseback	George Kaufman/ Marc Connelly
A Kiss in Xanadu	music by Deems Taylor

GRAND OPERA HOUSE
May 9, 1927 — September 4, 1927

The Road to Yesterday	Beulah Marie Dix/
	Evelyn Greenleaf Sutherland
Lazy Bones	Owen Davis
The Patsy	Barry Conners
The Poor Nut	J. C. and Elliott Nugent
*Charley**	J. C. and Elliott Nugent/
	Cliff Goldsmith
The Last of Mrs. Cheyney	Frederick Lonsdale
The Enemy	Channing Pollack
Pomeroy's Past	Clare Kummer
Kismet	Edward Knoblock
On Approval	Frederick Lonsdale
Applesauce	Barry Conners
Alias the Deacon	John Hymer/
	Leroy Clemens
The Wolf	Eugene Walters
The Show Off	George Kelly
Fu Manchu	Sax Rohmer
Beau Brummel	Clyde Fitch

May 14 — September 23, 1928
and September 24, 1928 — February 17, 1929

Saturday's Children	Maxwell Anderson
Why Marry	Jesse Lynch Williams
The Jest	Sam Benelli
Interference	Roland Fortune/
	Harold Deardon
Crime	Sam Shipman/
	John Humer
Her Cardboard Lover	Jacques Duval

117

Wooden Kimono	John Floyd
The Baby Cyclone	George M. Cohan
The Dover Road	A.A. Milne

TAFT AUDITORIUM

The Firebrand	Edwin Justus Mayer
The Copperhead	Augustus Thomas
The Play's the Thing	Ferenc Molnar
The Proud Princess	Dorothy Donnelly/ Richard Sheldon
Kempy	J. C. and Elliott Nugent
The Beautiful Adventure	de Flers/de Gaillavet
Broadway	Phillip Dunning/ George Abbott
The Purple Mask	Paul Armont/ Jean Manoussi
Mr. Antonio	Booth Tarkington
The Green Goddess	William Archer
The Butter and Egg Man	George S. Kaufman
Tommy	Howard Lindsay/ Bert Robinson
Loose Ankles	Sam Janney
The First Year	Frank Craven
Charm	John Kirkpatrick
Mrs. Wiggs of the Cabbage Patch	dramatized by Anne Flexner
Eva the Fifth	Kenyon Nicholson/ John Golden
The Gorilla	Ralph Spence
Tarnish	Gilbert Emery
Abie's Irish Rose	Anne Nichols
Easy Virtue	Noel Coward
The Ghost Train	Arnold Ridley
Too Many Husbands	Somerset Maugham
Treasure Island	adapter unknown

The Barker	Kenyon Nicholson
The Constant Wife	Somerset Maugham
The Big Pond	George Middleton/ A.E. Thomas
The Shannons of Broadway	James Gleason
Loose Ankles	Sam Janney

March 4, 1929 — June 16, 1929

The Proud Princess	Dorothy Donnelly/ Edward Sheldon
These Few Ashes	Leonard Ide
The Marriage Bed	Ernest Pascal
The Enchanted April	Kane Campbell
Deuces Wild	Sam Janney
Ned McCobb's Daughter	Sidney Howard
The Road to Rome	Robert Sherwood
The Outsider	Dorothy Brandon
Burlesque	George Waters/ Arthur Hopkins
Death Takes a Holiday	Alberto Casella
The High Road	Frederick Lonsdale
The Silver Cord	Sidney Howard
The Squall	Jean Dart

October 15, 1929 — May 4, 1930

Peter Ibbetson	George Du Maurier
Our Betters	Somerset Maugham
East of Suez	Somerset Maugham
Joneys	Ann Morrison/ John Peter Toohey
Silent House	John Brandon/ George Abbott
Ariadne	A.A. Milne

The Goose Hangs High	Lewis Beach
Holiday	Philip Barry
L'arlesienne	Alphonse Daudet
	(trans. Charles Livingood)
Enter Madame	Gilda Varesi/
	Dolly Byrne
The Wild Duck	Henrik Ibsen
The Silent House	John Brandon/
	George Pickett
The Perfect Alibi	A.A. Milne
The Bachelor Father	Edward Carpenter
The Wisdom Tooth	Marc Connelly
Little Women	Marion de Forest
Remote Control	Clyde North/
	Albert Fuller/
	Jack Nelson
Your Uncle Dudley	Howard Lindsay/
	Bertrand Robinson
The Youngest	Philip Barry
Secret Service	William Gillette
Let Us Be Gay	Rachel Crothers

1929-30 Apprentice company performances, free to subscribers:

Noah's Flood
A Christmas Mystery
Tom Til
Abraham and Isaac
The Very Naked Boy

Nevertheless
Jack and Joan
A Sunday Morning
Medicine Shop
St. George and the Dragon

October 21, 1930 — March 8, 1931

Rebound — Donald Ogden
The Stand By — Raymond Van Sickler
Those We Love — George Abbott
The Royal Family — George Kaufman/ Edna Ferber

Monna Vanna — Maurice Maeterlinck
The Apron — Dorena Davis
Little Accidents — Floyd Dell/ Thomas Mitchell

The Swan — Ferenc Molnar
Broken Dishes — Martin Flavin
Alice in Wonderland — adapter unknown
The Spider — unknown
The Torch Bearers — George Kelly
Solid South — Lawton Campbell
Fashion — Anna Cora Mowatt
It's A Wise Child — Laurie Johnson
Alimony for Albert — Gladys Angus
Maids Errant — Robert Housum
The Racket — Bartlet Cormack
Coquette — George Abbott

(Holliday Coll. CHS.)

*premiere

Bibliography

Abbreviations used in Works Cited:

SW Coll. Billy Rose ~ Stuart Walker Collection, in the Billy Rose Theatre Collection, The New York Public Library for the Performing Arts, Lincoln Center New York, New York

Holliday Coll. CHS ~ Joseph Holliday Collection, Cincinnati Historical Society, Museum Center, Cincinnati, Ohio

Margaret Herrick ~ Margaret Herrick Library, Academy of Motion Picture Arts and Sciences Center for Motion Picture Study, Beverly Hills, California

BOOKS

Bentley, Eric. *What is Theater?* New York: Antheneum, 1979.

Bierstadt, Edward Hale. *Dunsany the Dramatist.* Boston: Little Brown, 1917.

—. Introduction. *Portmanteau Plays.* By Stuart Walker. Cincinnati: Stewart Kidd, 1919. iii-xl.

—. Introduction. *More Portmanteau Plays.* By Stuart Walker. Cincinnati: Stewart Kidd, 1921. xv-xxx.

Bryant, Betty. *Here Comes the Showboat!* Kentucky: University Press of Kentucky, 1994.

Cheney, Sheldon. *The Art Theatre.* New York: Knopf, 1969.

Clark, Constance and Mari Kathleen Fielder. "Jessie Bonstelle." *Notable Women in the American Theatre*. Alice M. Robinson, Vera Mowry Roberts, and Milly S. Barranger, eds. New York: Greenwood, 1989. 76-82.

Colum, Padraic. Introduction. *A Dreamer's Tales and Other Stories*. By Lord Dunsany. New York: Boni & Liveright, 1917.

Dickinson, Thomas H. *The Insurgent Theatre*. New York: Huebash, 1917.

Dunsany, Edward John M.D.P. Preface. *The Last Book of Wonder*. 1916. New York: Books for Libraries, 1969.

Fergusson, Francis. "America Between the Wars." *The Human Image in Dramatic Literature*. New York: Doubleday, 1957. 5-22.

Gillespie, Richard C. *The James Adams Floating Theatre*. Maryland: Tidewater Publishers, 1991.

Hansen, Richard. "Walker Company." *American Theatre Companies 1888-1930*. Weldon B. Durham, ed. New York: Greenwood, 1987. 455-460.

Harris, Laurilyn J. "Hedgerow Theatre." *American Theatre Companies 1888-1930*. Weldon B. Durham, ed. New York: Greenwood, 1987. 212-220.

Havigurst, Walter. *River to the West*. New York: Putnam, 1970.

Mackay, Constance D'Arcy. *The Little Theatre in the United States*. New York: Holt, 1917.

Marker, Lise-Lone. *David Belasco: Naturalism in the American Theatre*. New Jersey: Princeton UP, 1975.

Menville, Douglas and R. Reginald, ed. *Dreamers of Dreams*.
New York: Arno Press, 1978.

Moses, Montrose J., ed., *Another Treasury of Plays for Children*.
Boston: Little Brown, 1926.

National Encyclopedia of American Biography. Vol 38.
New York: White & Co., 1953. 305-306.

Nordloh, David J., ed. *Augustus Thomas*.
Bloomington: Indiana University, 1984.

Quinlan, David. *The Illustrated Guide to Film Directors*.
London: Batsford, 1983.309-310.

Rankins, Walter. *Historic Augusta and Augusta College*.
Augusta: published by the author, 1949.

Rosten, Leo C. *Hollywood: The Movie Colony*.
New York: Harcourt, 1941.

Sayler, Oliver M. *Our American Theatre*.
New York: Brentano, 1923.

Storey, Margaret and Hugh Gillis. *Players' Nursery*.
Stanford: Dramatist's Alliance, 1940.

Styan, J.L. *Modern Drama in Theory and Practice. Volume 1:
Realism and Naturalism*. Cambridge: Cambridge UP, 1981.

Tarkington, Booth. *Seventeen*. New York. Harper Brothers, 1915.
Drama League Program. SW Coll. Billy Rose.

Trav, S.D. *No Applause — Just Throw Money*.
New York: Faber and Faber, 2005.

Walker, Stuart. *Portmanteau Plays*. Ed. with intro. by Edward Hale Bierstadt. Cincinnati: Stewart Kidd, 1919.

—. *More Portmanteau Plays*. Ed. with intro. by Edward Hale Bierstadt. Cincinnati: Stewart Kidd, 1921.

—. *Portmanteau Adaptations*. Ed. with intro. by Edward Hale Bierstadt. Cincinnati: Stewart Kidd, 1922.

Who Was Who In the Theatre: 1912-1976, Q-Z. 2475.

Yurka, Blanche. *Bohemian Girl*. Athens: Ohio UP, 1970.

Dissertations and Theses

Blaustein, Jane Elizabeth. "The Art Theater Movement in America as Recorded in Theater Arts Magazine 1916-1921." Thesis. U of California, Los Angeles, 1966.

Jackson, Richard Scott. "Stuart Walker and Company: Broadway in the Middle West." Thesis. Purdue U, 1958.

Shoup, Gail Leo, Jr., "The Pasadena Community Playhouse: Its Origins and History from 1917 to 1942." Diss. U of California, Los Angeles, 1968.

Newspapers and Periodicals

Abbey, Lorenzo. Untitled Clipping *Suburban Society Magazine* March, 1916. SW Coll. Billy Rose.

Adams, Carl. Untitled Clipping *Cincinnati Enquirer* February 4, 1930. Holliday Coll. CHS.

Alexander, Diane. "Pasadena Playhouse." Pasadena Today Magazine June 1985: 6-15.

"Baby Theatre Opens." New York Times July 15, 1915.
SW Coll. Billy Rose.

Baker, Colgate. "Seventeen, A Dispensation of Delight."
Saturday Review February 2, 1918. SW Coll. Billy Rose.

Baker, Tarkington. "From the Viewpoint of the Arctic."
Indianapolis Star August 1, 1918.

Barnes, Howard. Untitled Clipping *New York Journal Tribune*
March 9, no year. SW Coll. Billy Rose.

Bierstadt, Edward Hale. "Repertory Theater in America."
Brentano's Book Chat October, 1921. SW Coll. Billy Rose.

"*Birthday of the Infanta.*" *Detroit Journal* 1917.
SW Coll. Billy Rose.

Brooks, Katherine. Untitled Clipping. *Boston Evening Record*
February, 1916. SW Coll. Billy Rose.

Caldwell, Howard. "Summer Stock With Stuart Walker."
Indianapolis Magazine October 1976: 56-57.

Carr, Philip. Untitled Clipping. *New York Times* July 20,
1930. SW Coll. Billy Rose.

"Children of Institutions are Guests of Drama League."
Pittsburgh Dispatch November 11, 1916.

"The Chronicler." *Dayton News* January 14, 1917.
SW Coll. Billy Rose.

Clark, Norman. "Stuart Walker's Company Should Interest
Baltimore." *Baltimore News* January 28, 1924.

Collier, Carl, ed., *University Weekly News* March 2, 1903.
College-Conservatory of Music Library U of Cincinnati.

"Come Seven." *Indianapolis News* June 1921.
Indiana State Library, Reference Division.

"The Dummy." *Indianapolis Star* May 22, 1917.

"Dunsany in Gripsack." *New York Times* February 9, 1919.

Elliston, George. "Cincinnatian in Hollywood."
Cincinnati Times-Star May 23, 1938: 11.

"English's Has a Good One."
Indianapolis News August 13, 1918: 7.

"Fall Injures Walker." *Cincinnati Enquirer* circa 1935.
SW Coll. Billy Rose.

Fields, William A. "Stuart Walker, Noted Figure in American Theater, Will Head His Company in Final Play of Season."
Indianapolis Star August 28, 1927: Sec. 7:2.

"*Gaston Chevrolet* and *Two Kisses*."
Indianapolis Star June 1, 1920.

"George Allison Discusses the Future of Repertory Theater in the United States." *Detroit Herald* June 28, 1924.
SW Coll. Billy Rose.

Goldenburg, William Smith. "Amusements." *Cincinnati Enquirer* September 5, 1926. Holliday Coll. CHS.

— . "Curtain Down" *Cincinnati Enquirer* May 4, 1929.
Box 9 Folder 17. Holliday Coll. CHS.

——. "More On Strike." *Cincinnati Enquirer* October 13, 1929. Box 9 Holliday Coll. CHS.

——. "Theater." *Cincinnati Enquirer* September 16, 1926.

——. "Thief of Time." *Cincinnati Enquirer* November 24, 1929.

——. "Walker Season Closes." *Cincinnati Enquirer* September 5, 1926. Holliday Coll. CHS.

——. Untitled Clipping, *Cincinnati Enquirer* September 2, 1928. Box 9 Folder 7. Holliday Coll. CHS.

——. Untitled Clipping, *Cincinnati Enquirer* December 2, 1928. SW Coll. Billy Rose.

——. Untitled Clipping, *Cincinnati Enquirer* May 4, 1930. Box 9 Folder 15 Holliday Coll. CHS.

"*Great Expectations* Hit; Writing, Acting, Flawless." *Hollywood Reporter* October 10, 1934.

Hamilton, Clayton. Untitled Clipping, *Vanity Fair* March, 1918. SW Coll. Billy Rose.

Hermcheil, William. Untitled Clipping, *Indianapolis News* July 3, 1920: 15-16.

Hickman, Walter D. "Stuart Walker Blames the Press and Public." *Indianapolis Times* August 1, 1928.

Hines, Dixie. "Seamy Side of Broadway." *Cleveland Press* July 25, 1915.

Holliday, Joseph E. "Stuart Walker's Cincinnati Theater." *Cincinnati Historical Society Bulletin* 35, No. 3 Fall, 1977: 150-172.

Holmes, Ralph. "Back Stage Story." *Detroit Journal* July 30, 1921.

"*Honors Are Even.*" Indianapolis Star May 1, 1922.

"*Ibbetson.*" Indianapolis Star July 24, 1923.

"In Society." Cincinnati Enquirer April 30, 1929: 11. Holliday Coll. CHS.

"*Infanta.*" Indianapolis Star July 17, 1917.

"In the Wake of the Portmanteau Theatre." Cleveland Leader January 14, 1917.

"It Pays to Advertise." Indianapolis Star May 15, 1917.

Jennings, Paul. "Stuart Walker — A Cincinnati Institution." The Cincinnatian Magazine no month 1927: 8-9. Holliday Collection. CHS.

"Kismet." Indianapolis Star July 1, 1919.

"Let Mr. Walker's Company Start." Indianapolis Star Summer 1917. SW Coll. Billy Rose.

"Local Stock Companies are Gaining Importance Says Walker." Detroit Times December 10, 1924. SW Coll. Billy Rose.

"Lord Dunsany's Plays Staged by Stuart Walker." Christian Science Monitor November 21, 1916.

"Main Street." Theatre Magazine December 1921: 387.

McDermott, W. F. "Stuart Walker's Season in Retrospect." Indianapolis Star September 4, 1920: 8.

Morehouse, Ward. "Broadway After Dark." 1933.
Margaret Herrick.

Morris, Paul. "Lord Dunsany — A Soldier and Playwright."
The Theatre 25 (February 1917): 96-97.

"Mr. Walker Looks Back." *New York Times* February 7, 1932.

"*The Mystery of Edwin Drood.*" *Motion Picture Herald*
March 30, 1935. Stuart Walker file, Margaret Herrick.

Nathan, George Jean. "*Laughter of Gods* Groans 'Neath Big Load
of Walkerism." February 20, 1919. SW Coll. Billy Rose.

"October 17 Chosen as Date Walker Company Will Open."
Cincinnati Enquirer September 22, 1929. #1 Box 9.
Holliday Coll. CHS.

"Pictures: *Mystery of Edwin Drood.*" *Variety* March 27, 1935.
Stuart Walker file, Margaret Herrick.

Richardson, Katherine. "Drama League Speaker."
St. Louis Dispatch April 1916.

Sayler, Oliver M. "Lord Dunsany." *Boston Evening Transcript*
October 21, 1916. SW Coll. Billy Rose.

—. "Stuart Walker and His Theater." *New York Herald Tribune*
Item #126, Holliday Coll. CHS.

—. "Stuart Walker Bucks Two Proverbs." *New York Herald Tribune*
circa 1930. Box 10 Folder 8. Holliday Coll. CHS.

"*School for Scandal.*" *Indianapolis News* August 1, 1922.

"Season Closes." *Cincinnati Commercial Tribune* May 19, 1918. Box 10 Folder 9. Holliday Coll. CHS.

"*Seventeen* Will Make Its First Bow Tonight To Indianapolis Public." *Indianapolis Star* June 18, 1917.

"Show Shop." *Indianapolis Star* August 14, 1917.

Soanes, Wood. "Ex-Lumberjack Directs Screen Productions and Holds Class in Acting." Hollywood circa 1931. Stuart Walker file, Margaret Herrick.

"The Stage." *Baltimore Evening* Sun 1924. SW Coll. Billy Rose.

"Stage vs. Screen." *Cincinnati Times-Star.* June 25, 1927. SW Coll. Billy Rose.

Stiegler, William. "Stuart Walker Season Will Open." *Cincinnati Times* October 1929: 4.

Stiles, Hinton. "In the Glare of Calcium." *Providence Tribune* August 1, 1915.

"Stock Coming Back Opines J. J. Shubert." *Variety* September 28, 1923. SW Coll. Billy Rose.

"Stuart Walker Aims to Restore Youth to Theater." *Christian Science Monitor* February 14, 1916.

"Stuart Walker and Stock." *Cincinnati Enquirer.* Holliday Coll. CHS.

"Stuart Walker Discusses Stock Company." *Billboard Magazine* December 8, 1928: 104.

"Stuart Walker's Estate Left to Adopted Son."
Cincinnati Times-Star. April 29, 1941.

"Stuart Walker, Ex-Cincinnatian, Playwright and Movie Producer Dies in Beverly Hills." *Cincinnati Times-Star* March 14, 1941.

"Stuart Walker May Not Return." *Cincinnati Commercial Tribune* September 27, 1926.

"Stuart Walker, 53, Producer, is Dead." *New York Times* March, 14, 1941.

"Stuart Walker Has Summer Training School." *Cincinnati Sun* September 22, 1924.

"Stuart Walker Productions Fully Up to Thespian Standards of Broadway." *Dayton Journal* August 17, 1924. SW Coll. Billy Rose.

"Stuart Walker Rites Will Be Held Tuesday." *Cincinnati Times-Star.* March 17, 1941.

"Take Up Thy Theater and Walk." *Washington D.C. Herald* January 1916. SW Coll. Billy Rose.

"Talk of Modern Stagecraft." *Buffalo Express* May 14, 1915. SW Coll. Billy Rose.

"Teaching Children to Know Drama." *New York Times* May 11, 1924. SW Coll. Billy Rose.

"Theater Too Elaborate; Mr. Walker Predicts Return to Simplicity." *Boston Advisor* February 11, 1916.

"The Theaters." *Cincinnati Enquirer* April 12, 1925. Holliday Coll. CHS.

Thompson, Glenn. "Stuart Walker Homesick; Follows Reds Progress." *Cincinnati Enquirer* March 12, 1939: 3-4.

Thuman, J. H. "Theater." *Cincinnati Enquirer* April 21, 1918. Box 10 Folder 9, Holliday Coll. CHS.

"Time." *Cincinnati Enquirer* September 18, 1923. SW Coll. Billy Rose.

"Time." *New York Times* December 1923. SW Coll. Billy Rose.

Towse, Ranken. "*Job.*" *New York Evening Post* May 17, 1919.

Tucker, Robert G. "Closing — Stuart Walker Season." *Indianapolis Star*. August 5, 1928.

— . "The Silver Fox." *Indianapolis Star* July 30, 1922.

— . "Mr. Walker's Tenth Season Opening at Keith's Monday." *Indianapolis Star* May 6, 1928, Sec. 7.

— . "Stuart Walker, Producer Dies; Launched His First Stock Company in This City." *Indianapolis Star* March 14, 1941.

— . Untitled Article *Indianapolis Star* March 25, 1923, Sec. 6.

Untitled advertisement, *Cincinnati Enquirer*. November 10, 1929. Box 9 Folder 15. Holliday Coll. CHS.

Untitled Clipping, *Cleveland Press* SW Coll. Billy Rose.

Untitled Clipping, *Columbus Journal* December 17, 1916. SW Coll. Billy Rose.

Untitled Clipping, *Indianapolis Star* September, 1923.
  Indiana State Library Reference Division, item #100-730.

Untitled Clipping, *Los Angeles* Examiner March 14, 1941.
  SW Coll. Billy Rose.

Untitled Clipping. *Munsey's Magazine* October, 1915.
  Indiana State Library Reference Division.

Untitled Clipping. *New York Evening Weekly* April 30, 1917.
  SW Coll. Billy Rose.

Untitled Clipping. *New York Morning Telegraph* December 1, 1923.
  SW Coll. Billy Rose.

Untitled Clipping. *Sigma Chi Magazine* SW Coll. Billy Rose.

Untitled Clipping. *Theater Arts Magazine* circa 1917.
  SW Coll. Billy Rose.

"Walker Peeved." *Variety* August 18, 1922. SW Coll. Billy Rose.

"Walker Planned to Reproduce Steamboat Cabin in His Home."
  Cincinnati Times-Star March 18, 1941.

"Walker Players as a Local Enterprise."
  Cincinnati Commercial Tribune June 2, 1922.

"Walker Players at Strand." *Huntington Dispatch/Advisor*
  October 27, 1926. SW Coll. Billy Rose.

Walker, Stuart. "Genesis of the Portmanteau."
  The Theatre 29 (April 1919): 207.

Walker, Stuart. "The Spirit of Youth Behind the Footlights." *Theatre Magazine* February 1918 27:75-76.

Warsden, Rancholt. "Little Theatre and Big Ideas." *Theatre Magazine* 25 (February 1917): 92.

"Wedding Bells." *Indianapolis Star* August 7, 1921.

"Why Go to the Theater?" *Pittsburgh Post* December 24, 1916. SW Coll. Billy Rose.

White, Matthew, Jr. "The Stage." *Munsey's Magazine* (October 1915): SW Coll. Billy Rose.

Whitworth, Walter. "Stuart Walker's Disciples." *Indianapolis News* June 17, 1922.

"Work That Stage Folk Are Doing for the War." *New York City World* February 10, 1918. SW Coll. Billy Rose.

LETTERS

Gaul, George. Letter to Percy Hammond: "Oddiments and Remainders." 1924. SW Coll. Billy Rose.

McSweeney, Meg. Letter to the author. January 24, 1996.

Walker, Stuart. Letter to Robert Black. September 28, 1931. #199 Holliday Coll. CHS.

— . Letter to Beulah Bondi. December 15, 1924. Beulah Bundy file. Margaret Herrick.

— . Letter to the editor. *Indianapolis Star*. October 12, 1922. SW Coll. Billy Rose.

—. Letter to Robert Garland. August 20, 1931. SW Coll. Billy Rose.

—. Letter to Hubert Osborne. Spring, 1931. SW Coll. Billy Rose.

—. Letter to Oliver M. Sayler. November 13, 1930. SW Coll. Billy Rose.

—. Letter to Oliver M. Sayler. November 23, 1930. SW Coll. Billy Rose.

—. Letter to Oliver M. Sayler. November 30, 1930. SW Coll. Billy Rose.

—. Letter to Oliver M. Sayler. September 15, 1931. SW Coll. Billy Rose.

—. Letter to Robert Tucker of *Indianapolis Star*. November 23, 1923. SW Coll. Billy Rose.

Wyatt, Jane. Letter to the author. March 9, 1996.

INTERVIEWS

Anderson, Jean Jory. Telephone interview. November 27, 1995.

Jory, Jon. Telephone interview. November 18, 1995.

—. Telephone interview. December 11, 1995.

Nimitz, Ruth. Telephone interview. December 28, 1995.

Zemsky, Dr. David. Telephone interview. December 28, 1995.

Miscellaneous

Actors Guild memorial program. May 28, 1941. SW Coll. Billy Rose.

American Academy of Dramatic Arts Audition Record Book, April 3, 1908. Pages 178-179 signed by Franklin Haven Sargent.

Box Office Report. Cincinnati Grand Theatre, circa 1917. SW Coll. Billy Rose.

Cincinnatian. University of Cincinnati Yearbook, 1899 to 1903. College-Conservatory of Music Library. U of Cincinnati.

Cincinnati Chamber of Commerce program. January 27, 1925. SW Coll. Billy Rose.

Kander, John and Fred Ebb. *New York, New York.* United Artists, 1977.

Kidd Dramatic Publications flyer. SW Coll. Billy Rose.

National Council of Teachers of English. "A Study Guide to Dickens' *Great Expectations.*" Holland Roberts, Publications Chairman. Chicago, 1934. Stuart Walker file. Margaret Herrick.

Paramount Public Corporation Press Sheets, 1931-1933. Stuart Walker file. Margaret Herrick.

Paramount Studios unpublished press release #19986. Stuart Walker file. Margaret Herrick.

Paramount Studios unpublished press release #175335. Stuart Walker file. Margaret Herrick.

Paramount Studios Western Union Press Release.
 Signed by Earl Wingart. March 5, 1931.
 Stuart Walker file. Margaret Herrick.

Portmanteau Publicity flyer. February, circa 1917.
 SW Coll. Billy Rose.

"Study Guide to Photoplay Studies of *Seventeen*."
 Vol 6, #11 Educational and Recreational Guide.
 Hollywood, 1940. SW Coll. Billy Rose.

Walker Cincinnati Company promotional flyer.
 Theatre folder Misc. 3. Holliday Coll. CHS.

Washington Square Players program. September 18, 1915.
 SW Coll. Billy Rose.

ACKNOWLEDGMENTS

I am grateful to all those who shared this adventure with me: first of all to my husband Alan for his support, his suggestions and his good humor; to Dr. Margaret Knapp for her love of theatrical history; to the late Lois Greene who first brought Stuart Walker to my attention; to Gary Moore, former Director of the Herberger Theater Center who gave me the flexibility to do the initial research; and, of course, to Steven Swerdfeger, publisher of Star Cloud Press.

Many thanks to Louis Botto, Senior Editor of PLAYBILL and author of IN THIS THEATER; Judy Kaye, Tony-award winning actress from PHANTOM OF THE OPERA, SOUVENIR, MAMA MIA and RAGTIME; John Holly, Western Regional Director of Actors' Equity; and Jessica L. Andrews, Executive Director of the Arizona Theatre Company who were kind enough to read the manuscript and offer their comments. These professionals represent the best of the legitimate theater in the Twenty-first Century.

In addition I would like to thank: The Tongret family of Augusta, Kentucky; Kathleen Conry, New York City; Anne B. Shepherd and Linda Bailey of the Cincinnati Historical Society; Mark Palkovic and Kevin Grace, University of Cincinnati Conservatory of Music Library; Martha E. Wright, Reference Librarian, Indiana State Library; Meg McSweeney, Assistant to the President, American Academy of Dramatic Arts; Jean Jory Anderson, Atascadero, California; Jon Jory, former Executive Producer, Actors Theatre of Louisville; Bob Taylor, Mary Ellen Rogan and Barbara Knowles at the Billy Rose Collection, New York Library for the Performing Arts Lincoln Center; Jackie Demaline, Cincinnati Enquirer; Jane Wyatt, Los Angeles, California; Mark Fleming, William Morris Talent Agency, Beverly Hills, California; Michael R. Roediger, Marketing, Victoria Theatre, Dayton, Ohio; Faye Thompson, Margaret Herrick Library, Acadmey of Motion Picture Arts and Sciences, Beverly Hills, California; Helen Rowin, Librarian, Music and Performing Arts, Detroit Public Library; Kathy Krzys, Special Collections, Hayden Library Arizona State University; the Herberger College of Fine Arts, Arizona State University; and Kathy Garner, Purdue University Library, West Lafayette, Indiana.

Lastly, thanks to Elia, Charlie & Lydia.

About the Author

JoAnn Yeoman started writing about theater in New York City where she wrote articles and interviews for publications that included Playbill, Grit, Dramatics, Key, CNS Wire Service of Canada and People, Places & Parties. Her fiction includes the plays: *Under the Broom Tree, The Manhattan Papers, And Lead Us Not Into Penn Station*, and *The Little Mischief* as well as the short stories: *Pas de Trois* and *Borders*.

JoAnn comes by her passion for and knowledge of theater quite honestly. She has performed and choreographed in theaters throughout the country including New York's Lincoln Center, Playwright's Horizon, Brooklyn Academy of Music, Cincinnati Conservatory's *Hot Summer Nights,* St. Luke's Chamber Opera in NYC, and for the Royal Viking Cruise Ship Lines. Her Musical Theater production, *No Legs,* tours to school districts and presents a "living history" of the American Musical by recreating landmark Broadway choreography within the context of developing styles. She has worked professionally with such personalities as Michael Bennett, Larry Fuller, Shirley Jones, Buddy Ebsen, JoAnne Worley, John Raitt, John Cullum, Nick Nolte and Ray Walston.

A Professor of Practice at Arizona State University, JoAnn teaches Musical Theater, Stage Movement, Acting, Broadway Dance, Period Dance, Auditioning, and Musicals on Film, and can currently be heard on KBAQ(89.5) as the "voice" of *ASU in Concert*. She also travels to universities giving workshops and master classes in choreographic style, musical theater history, and "survival" in the business of theater. JoAnn is a member of Actors Equity Association, Screen Actors Guild and the Society of Stage Directors and Choreographers.

She is married to playwright and novelist Alan Tongret and lives in Phoenix, Arizona with their dog, Puck and their cat, Bunthorne.

INDEX

Academy of Motion Picture Arts and Sciences, Margaret Herrick	27, 90, 96, 97, 121, 128, 129, 130, 134, 136, 139
Actors Equity Association	34, 142
Actors Guild	135, 142
American Academy of Dramatic Arts	7, 8, 84, 85, 135, 139
American Little Theater Movement	17
Anderson, Jean Jory	32, 43, 90, 91, 135, 139
As You Like It	7, 8
Arlen, Richard	76
Arliss, George	64
Augusta, Kentucky	I, 1, 2, 3, 6, 47, 64, 78, 84, 123, 139
Barry, Philip	70, 119
Belasco, David	11, 12, 13, 27, 36, 42, 45, 56, 76, 103, 107, 114, 115, 122
Bellevue, Kentucky	78
Beverly Hills, California	27, 48, 78, 98, 121, 130
Bierstadt, E. H.	29, 30, 86, 87, 89, 121, 123, 124, 125
Birthday of the Infanta, The	21, 36, 80, 88, 103, 125, 128
Black, Robert L.	69, 71, 80, 96, 134
Bluebird, The	19, 64
Bohemian Girl, The	4, 43, 91, 124
Boicourt, Marie	34
Bonstelle, Jessie	11, 12, 13, 20, 56, 57, 60, 61, 70, 85, 93, 122
Book of Job, The	36, 37, 38, 44, 104
Booth, Shirley	60
Booth Theater	40, 41
Bondi, Beulah	39, 46, 65, 72, 90, 134
Bottomley, Gordon	21
Boyd, William	76
Brown, Gilmor	60
Bryant's Showboat	3
Bulldog Drummond	76

Buffalo, New York	12, 13
Byington, Spring	44, 63
Candida	65, 66, 94, 108, 115
Carnegie Hall	10, 38
Chapman, William	3, 84
Cheney, Sheldon	59
Christadora Settlement House	16, 18, 31, 86
Cincinnati Grand Theatre	25, 88, 135
Cincinnati Historical Society	27, 96, 121, 127, 139
Cincinnati, Ohio	32, 33, 36, 45, 46, 47, 56, 57, 61, 62, 63, 65, 68, 70, 72
Cohan's Revue	25
Cohen, Octavius Roy	44, 106, 113, 116
Colbert, Claudette	76
Come Seven	44, 63, 106, 113, 116, 125
Commedia d'ell Arte	18
Cooper, Gary	74
Cooper, Jackie	79
Covington, Kentucky	5, 11
Cowl, Jane	64
Cox, James Governor	46
Cox Theatre	61, 62, 63, 66, 82, 94, 113
Cribbs, Mr. & Mrs. George Dent	68, 69
Crier by Night	21
Dayton, Ohio	46, 47, 56, 139
de Mille, Henry	9
Dean, Alexander	56
Dee, Frances	74
Death Takes a Holiday	70, 119
December Bride	44
Deeter, Jasper	60
Detroit Civic Theatre	13, 60, 93
Dickens, Charles	76
"disciples"	31, 32, 33, 134

Drama League	16, 20, 29, 85, 88, 123, 125
Dunsany, Lord	
(Edward John Moreton Drax Plunkett)	22, 23, 24, 41, 46, 87, 91, 104, 107, 114, 121, 122, 126, 128, 129
Eagle and the Hawk, The	76, 79
Ebb, Fred	28, 89, 136
Electra	11
Elser, Max Jr.	20, 27
English's Vaudeville House	40
False Madonna	76
Fan and Two Candlesticks, A	21
Field, Betty	79
Foster, Stephen	2, 64
Francis, Kaye	76
French, Augustus	3
Friedlander, Edgar	69
Gammer Gurton's Needle	21, 26
Garrick Theatre	12, 60
Gaul, George	33, 40, 42, 44, 46, 63, 91, 134
Geer, Will	60
Girl of the Golden West, The	45, 63, 107, 114
Girl of the Underworld, A	3
Gillette, William	70, 119
Gods of the Mountain, The	21, 107
Golden Doom, The	21, 23
Goldenburg, William	56, 66, 67, 69, 93, 95, 126
Goodspeed Opera House	64
Gordon, Ruth	21, 35, 43, 44
Gowing, Almarin	44
Graham, Joseph	78
Grand Opera House	62, 66, 70, 116
Grant, Cary	74, 76
Great Expectations	76, 77, 97, 127, 136

Hale, Alan	76
Hanna, Arthur	69
Harvard	9
Hedgerow Theatre	60, 122
Heitland, Wilmot	17
Hickman, Walter D.	47, 92, 127
Holstein, Harold	39
Honors Are Even	62, 92, 106, 113, 127
Hull, Henry	76
Ibsen, Henrik	21, 70, 119
Indianapolis, Indiana	13, 31, 33, 35, 36, 37, 38, 40, 41, 42, 43, 44, 45, 46, 47, 48, 56, 62, 63, 67, 68, 71, 101
Hoop-La	6
It Pays to Advertise	34, 103, 128
Janney, Russell	20, 27
Jazz Singer, The	66
Jonathan Makes a Wish	41, 104, 107
Jory, Jean Spurney	32, 43
Jory, Jon	32, 43, 57, 58, 91, 93, 135, 139
Jory, Victor	32, 43, 57, 58, 72
Joslin, Allen R.	69
Jubilee Singers	7, 63
Kander, John	28, 89, 136
Kanin, Garson	35
Kelly, Gregory	33, 35, 43, 44
King Argimines and the Unknown Warrior	21
Kismet	42, 91, 104, 108, 116, 128
Klaw and Erlanger	12
L'arlesienne	69, 70, 119
Lady of the Weeping Willow Tree	21, 26
La Jolla Playhouse	64
Latimer, Grace	44

Lasky, Jesse L.	75
Laughton, Charles	76
Lead Pencil Club	6
Lewis, Sinclair	44
Lincoln Center Library of Performing Arts	27
Little Women	70, 119
Livingood, Charles J.	69, 119
Lombard, Carole	76
Lowe, Edmund	76
Lowry, Judith	33, 65
Louisville, Kentucky	42, 45, 56
Lyric Theater	62
Lyceum Theatre School of Acting	9
MacDonald, Donald	65
MacMillan, Mary	21
McNauff, Des	64
Mackay, Constance D'Arcy	17, 68, 86, 122
Madame X	65, 114
Main Street	44, 65, 94, 95, 106, 128
Major, Clare Tree	64
Materlinck, Maurice	19
March, Frederic	76
Marshall, Herbert	76
Maude, Beatrice	34
Maugham, Somerset	69, 105, 113, 116, 118, 119
Medicine Show, The	80
Merrick, David	34, 64
Miller, George	7
Minstrel Show	3, 44
Misleading Lady	76, 104
Monna Vanna	44, 106, 114, 120
Moscow Art Players	19

Morris, McKay	42, 45, 46, 65, 68
Mrs. Wiggs of the Cabbage Patch	66, 118
Murat Theater	33, 34, 36, 41, 46, 47, 61, 63, 103
My Old Kentucky Home	2
Mystery of Edwin Drood, The	76, 96, 97, 129
National Council of Teachers of English	77, 136
Neighborhood Playhouse	28
Nevertheless	9, 80, 103, 106, 120
Nimitz, Ruth	82, 99, 135
New Sensation	3
New York City	8, 13, 16, 28, 29, 31, 35, 36, 37, 38, 40, 41, 44, 45, 46, 48, 64, 65, 70, 72, 80
Nicholas, J. K.	39
Ohio River	1, 3, 84
Our Betters	69, 119
Our Little Wife	63, 106
Paramount Pictures	74, 75, 76, 78, 96, 97, 136
Pasadena Playhouse	60, 124
Patterson, Elizabeth	44, 46, 47, 66, 73
Peter Ibbetson	45, 68, 107, 119
Portmanteau Theatre	14, 15, 16, 17, 18, 19, 20, 21, 22, 23, 24, 25, 26, 27, 28, 29, 30, 31, 36, 41, 42, 46, 59, 80, 81, 82, 85, 86, 87, 88, 121, 123, 124, 128, 133, 136
Princess Theater	29, 41
Provincetown Players	28
Rathbone, Basil	60, 65, 73
Revere, Anne	60
Rains, Claude	76
Reed, Charley	39
Reed, Florence	69, 76
Ripley, Ohio	1
Rogers, Agnes	33
Rooney, Mickey	79

Ross, Lillian	34
Rosten, Leo	75, 78, 97, 98, 123
Sayler, Oliver	33, 37, 67, 87, 89, 90, 95, 123, 129, 134, 135
Sargent, Franklin Haven	9, 85, 135
School for Scandal, The	44, 45, 91, 107, 115, 129
Scott, Randolph	74
Secret Service	70, 119
Seventeen	25, 29, 35, 41, 43, 65, 79, 90, 103, 123, 124, 129, 136
Shakespeare, William	9, 15, 20, 85
Sheafe, William J.	17
Shubert, J. J.	12, 13, 63, 68, 70, 94, 130
Shubert, Lee	70
Shulberg, B.P.	74
Sing Me a Love Song	77
Six Who Pass While the Lentils Boil	21, 26, 67, 103, 106
Sir David Wears a Crown	67, 106
Slidell, Louisiana	7
Smilin' Through	44, 105, 107, 114, 115
Somnes, George	56, 68
Southern Creosoting Company	7
Stage Women's War Relief	25
Stair, E. D.	12
Stair-Havilland Circuit	12
Stanislavski, Constantin	12, 19
Stewart Kidd Dramatic Publications	26, 86, 87, 88, 121, 123, 124, 136
Stevenson, William	21
Strindberg, August	21
Storey, Margaret	13, 60, 85, 123
Stuart, Marshall	11
Stuart Walker Orchestra Ensemble	68
Taft, Anna	69, 71
Taft Theater	62, 68
Talbot, Ona B.	33, 34

Tarkington, Booth	35, 103, 104, 108, 114, 117, 123, 125
Taymor, Julie	19
Thomas, Augustus	11, 85, 109, 117, 123
Time	46, 64, 89, 131, 132
Treasure Island	67, 118
Trimplet, The	21, 106
Tucker, Robert	46, 79, 92, 135
Two Kisses	42, 105, 106, 126
University of Cincinnati	5, 7, 9
University Comedy Club	6
Universal Pictures	76, 77
Varsity Minstrels	6
Vaudeville	3, 40, 41, 84
Very Naked Boy, The	80, 103, 120
Victoria Theatre	46
Walker, Arthur Helm	48, 97
Walker, Cliff	5
Walker, Matilda Taliaferro Armstrong	3
Ward, Mrs. Coonley	16
White Woman	76
Wild Duck, The	70, 119
Wilde, Oscar	21, 36, 107, 114
Wood, Peggy	60, 65, 106
Woodward High School	5
Wray, Johnny	63, 109
Wyatt, Jane	76, 77, 97, 135
Woman, The	36, 76, 103
You Can Never Tell	36
Youngest, The	70, 119
Yurka, Blanche	42, 43, 44, 45, 63, 70, 91, 124
Zemsky, Dr. David	82, 99, 135
Zimmerer, Frank J.	17, 33, 39

SINGULARITY PRESS

-an imprint of Star Cloud Press-

The Inn of a Thousand Days
written and illustrated by ALAN TONGRET
Cloth, 296 pages — $ 24.95 (USA)

ISBN: 0-9765711-0-2

"I have reader Alan Tongret's memoir with absolute fascination; it is surely one of the most harrowing accounts of obsession since Moby Dick. In this case the Great White Whale was a hotel.... Tongret's account is more than merely a suspenseful story; it carries implied questions of character and commitment, and how they may be most wisely fulfilled."— from the Foreword by Dale Wasserman

"...*The Inn of a Thousand Days* is simply terrific." — Ron Carlson

www.StarCloudPress.com

www.ingramcontent.com/pod-product-compliance
Lightning Source LLC
LaVergne TN
LVHW011421080426
835512LV00005B/190